Comments on other *Amazing Stories* from readers & reviewers

"*Tightly written volumes filled with lots of wit and humour about famous and infamous Canadians.*"
Eric Shackleton, *The Globe and Mail*

"*The heightened sense of drama and intrigue, combined with a good dose of human interest is what sets* Amazing Stories *apart.*"
Pamela Klaffke, *Calgary Herald*

"*This is popular history as it should be... For this price, buy two and give one to a friend.*"
Terry Cook, a reader from Ottawa, on *Rebel Women*

"*Glasner creates the moment of the explosion itself in graphic detail...she builds detail upon gruesome detail to create a convincingly authentic picture.*"
Peggy McKinnon, *The Sunday Herald*, on *The Halifax Explosion*

"*It was wonderful...I found I could not put it down. I was sorry when it was completed.*"
Dorothy F. from Manitoba on *Marie-Anne Lagimodière*

"*Stories are rich in description, and bristle with a clever, stylish realness.*"
Mark Weber, *Central Alberta Advisor*, on *Ghost Town Stories II*

"*A compelling read. Bertin...has selected only the most intriguing tales, which she narrates with a wealth of detail.*"
Joyce Glasner, *New Brunswick Reader*, on *Strange Events*

"*The resulting book is one readers will want to share with all the women in their lives.*"
Lynn Martel, *Rocky Mountain Outlook*, on *Women Explorers*

ONTARIO MURDERS

AMAZING STORIES

ONTARIO MURDERS
Mysteries, Scandals, and
Dangerous Criminals

HISTORY/CRIME
by Susan McNicoll

For Catherine
I may have had the goal,
but you showed me the path
and I am eternally grateful

PUBLISHED BY ALTITUDE PUBLISHING CANADA LTD.
1500 Railway Avenue, Canmore, Alberta T1W 1P6
www.altitudepublishing.com
1-800-957-6888

Extreme care has been taken to ensure that all information presented in
this book is accurate and up to date. Neither the author nor the
publisher can be held responsible for any errors.

Publisher	Stephen Hutchings
Associate Publisher	Kara Turner
Series Editor	Jill Foran
Editor	Georgina Montgomery
Digital photo colouration & map	Scott Manktelow

We acknowledge the financial support of the Government
of Canada through the Book Publishing Industry Development
Program (BPIDP) for our publishing activities.

Altitude GreenTree Program
Altitude Publishing will plant twice as many trees as were used
in the manufacturing of this product.

National Library of Canada Cataloguing in Publication Data
McNicoll, Susan
Ontario murders / Susan McNicoll.

(Amazing stories)
Includes bibliographical references.
ISBN 1-55153-951-9

1. Murder--Ontario--History. I. Title. II. Series:
Amazing stories (Canmore, Alta.)

HV6535.C32O65 2004   364.152'3'09713   C2004-901176-6

An application for the trademark for Amazing Stories™
has been made and the registered trademark is pending.

Printed and bound in Canada by Friesens
4 6 8 9 7 5

Contents

Prologue

The light rain had stopped, but the area was still wet and pools of water — in addition to fallen trees and decades of swamp muck — impeded the young man's path through Blenheim Swamp. The February sky was overcast, making it darker than it should have been for midday, and the temperature hovered just above freezing.

Smoking a cigar as he made his way along the trail, the young man hardly seemed to notice the cold. And he certainly had no reason to fear the person who walked a few paces behind.

The bullet hit him with such a jolt that the cigar flew out of his mouth and his cigar case was knocked from his pocket.

The gunman walked over to the body, now lying motionless on the ground. He reached down and fired a second bullet into the head. It was unnecessary. The young man was already dead.

The murderer emptied the victim's pockets and then methodically cut the identifying labels off every piece of clothing on the body. He ripped the stiff collar from the dead man's neck with so much force that a piece of the linen shirt came with it. He left nothing on the body that could lead to its identification.

His plan was to drag the corpse along the path to Pine Pond and there sink it into oblivion. As he looked around, however, he could not find the trail he remembered from a year ago. Then, figuring the body would never be found anyway out in this desolate swamp, he settled for concealing it among the tangled thickets.

So confident was the murderer as he walked away that he didn't notice the cigar case even as he stepped on it. Handwritten on it was F.C. Benwell.

Chapter 1
Stolen Lives

he autumn of 1918 was turning into winter, and Mary McAuliffe was still seriously ill with the flu. When it turned into pneumonia, she was forced to spend time in bed even though she had two small children to look after — Irene, who was a couple of years old, and Herbie, only 10 months. The ailing woman would tuck the children in on either side of her while she lay suffering in bed.

One day, Mary was found with Irene and Herbie still lying next to her. Best estimates said she had been dead for two or three days.

It was a tough start in life for both children, and little Herbie's life in particular was never to get much easier.

* * *

June 21, 1950, was a hot, sunny day in the small Ontario village of Langton, located 19 kilometres southwest of Simcoe in the middle of the tobacco belt. It was 2:45 p.m., and the Imperial Bank of Canada, the only bank in town for Langton's 250 residents, was empty except for five employees and one customer, Frank Hall.

Suddenly a man walked in, brandishing a long-barrelled revolver. He was dressed in a dark blue suit coat, dark pants, and a dirty blue and white striped shirt. He also wore a sun helmet and dark sunglasses, which didn't conceal the stubble of a red beard.

"This is a stick-up!" he shouted. "Get in the corner and face the wall!"

The gunman then produced another weapon, an automatic pistol, and motioned to Lavona Leedham to leave her teller's cage and join the others at the back of the room. Before she complied with the order, Lavona tripped the bank's alarm. It was hooked up to a general store and gas station owned by Lombert VanHooren. He was supposed to order a roadblock when the buzzer rang in his garage. However, knowing the bank staff often just tested the alarm, VanHooren chose instead just to wander up to tell them it was working fine. When the robber saw him looking in the window, he beckoned VanHooren into the bank with the gun.

By that time, the bank manager, Arthur Beattie, and four more customers had entered the bank and were herded together with the others. The robber handed Frank Hall a shopping bag and ordered him to fill it with money from a drawer in the teller's cage. After that, Hall was ordered to open a cash box and put the money from it into the bag as well. When he opted to transfer the whole thing to the shopping bag, the box tore a hole in the bag and went right through to the floor.

The robber swore and handed Hall another bag. "Put the cash in there!" he yelled at Hall, "and, God damn, don't put the box in!"

The robber next turned to the bank's accountant, Henry Thompson, and told him to enter the vault and turn off the safe combinations so they could be opened. Thompson told him only the manager had the combination.

"At that time he said to me, 'Now listen, chum. I will be back to Langton, and I will kill you because I don't intend to get caught,'" Thompson later recalled.

Taking the threat seriously, Thompson turned off the upper combination of the outer door of the safe. He opened the outer door, but again told the gun-wielding stranger that he couldn't go any further because he didn't have the combination for the inner compartment. Thompson was threatened a second time.

"I finally told him that Mrs. Leedham had the other combination," Thompson stated. "The next thing I saw was

Mrs. Leedham entering the vault and she turned off her combination of the upper compartment in the safe."

The robber handed Thompson the bag, which was already partially filled with money, and told him to fill it with the bills and the silver coins stashed in the upper compartment. That task complete, everyone was ordered inside the vault.

When the robber had trouble closing the inner doors of the vault, he had to ask Thompson for assistance. "And hurry up if you don't want a sore head!" he warned the beleaguered accountant.

Things were starting to go awry for the thief. He had trouble locking the outer vault door and, after struggling with it for a while, was forced to leave it closed but unlocked.

It was 3.00 p.m. by the time the bank robber dashed out of the building with $22,575.17. He had a car waiting with the engine running. The black Ford Meteor, it was later learned, had been stolen in Windsor earlier in the week. The thief carried the bag of money in his arms, but just as he reached the car, the bottom of this bag also gave way. The frantic man threw what remained of the bag's contents into the car and hurriedly scooped up the bills lying on the road, shoving them into his pockets. At this point, the bank manager's wife happened to look out the window of their apartment above the bank. After watching the strange scene in the street below, she immediately wrote down the licence number of the car as it drove off.

Meanwhile, the group left behind in the vault realized quickly that the door was not locked and they ventured out into the bank. Two of them, Arthur Lierman and William Goddyn, ran out to Lierman's light blue Plymouth with the intention of following the robber.

A high-speed car chase ensued, covering a distance of just over 14 kilometres. The pursuit was witnessed by a number of people. As the cars sped along Kinglake Road, a resident by the name of A. Kyle observed the end of a gun extending from the passenger-side window of the second car. Another resident, Harry Manary, said the vehicles were travelling very fast, and that he distinctly heard two shots fired seven or eight seconds apart.

After a sharp turn in the road, the cars came into view of two men hoeing tobacco in a field. The youngest man, 16-year-old Robert Nobels, heard a shot and looked up as the two vehicles approached. He then saw the leading car come to a sudden stop in the ditch and the second car pull up behind it.

"A man was in the second car," Nobels later recalled, "and had his rifle out the window, and then I heard a shot and that man with a rifle dropped it and fell inside the car."

Nobels ducked to the ground. When he looked up, he saw a man walk around the cars and stop at the passenger side of the second vehicle. After hearing four or five more shots, Nobels crawled out of the field to get home. The other young man working in the field was farther away from the road, but he still managed to see someone going over the fence and disappearing into the bushes.

Constable W.E. Rogers was the first police officer to see the bullet-ridden bodies of Goddyn and Lierman in the front seat of Lierman's car. In the back seat was the rifle. Rogers said it was not loaded and would not fire or discharge a cartridge. A sun helmet, dark glasses, a .38 calibre revolver, and $21,289.45 were found in the robber's car.

In no time, the largest manhunt in Ontario's history to that point was launched. More than 100 officers descended on the area, and a bloodhound named Dr. Keen was brought up from Michigan to help in the search. The surrounding terrain into which the suspect escaped was perfect for hiding in, with thick woods, reforested sections, and valleys. Even the cultivated areas were covered in big, leafy tobacco plants.

Day One would go to the hunted man, who remained undetected. However, in a field 365 metres from the shooting, officers did find a shirt and a badly torn blue coat. A Thompson submachine gun also turned up nearby, hidden in some bushes.

The police kept up the search through the night and into Day Two, now without the bloodhound. As Day Three dawned, authorities began to wonder if the robber-turned-suspected-killer had managed to elude them permanently. But that evening, a farmer in Straffordville, 10 kilometres north of the murder scene, reported finding a man sleeping in the hayloft of his barn. Hearing the description of the intruder, the police realized it was the robber.

As the 100 officers moved to seal off the wooded area near the barn, a blinding hail and thunderstorm moved in. An Ontario Provincial Police officer then sent his entire 200-man force in to set up a tight cordon of the area. It took another 24 hours before the killer was finally flushed out of the bush.

"The man arrested was in an extreme state of exhaustion with about four or five days' growth of beard," trial judge Justice R.W. Treleaven later wrote in his summation of the trial. "His trousers were torn and, although without a shirt or undershirt, he was wearing an old suit coat." The suspect was covered in mosquito bites and had been badly scratched by the underbrush. In the pockets of the coat he had stolen the day before were some potatoes he had also stolen. He was taken to the Simcoe County Jail where he ate, bathed, shaved, and slept.

The next morning, the prisoner was placed in a line-up of 15 men. Of the 10 witnesses, nine positively identified him as the man who had robbed the bank. To this point, the prisoner had not said a word. On being cautioned and charged with murder, he was again asked his name. This time he replied, "Frank West will do."

His fingerprints were taken and an expert was quickly able to determine they matched the ones found inside the lead vehicle in the car chase. The suspect refused to sign a form accompanying the fingerprints.

On June 26, the reason for his reluctance to supply a name became clear. The RCMP matched Frank West's prints with a police record for someone using the aliases Fred Walker and George Walker. In 1938, the man had received a prison sentence of one month in Brantford, Ontario, for an attempted break and enter. A few months later, in Woodstock, he had been given a six-month sentence for a break and enter including theft.

A photograph of the robber, now calling himself Walker, was published in the paper. A Windsor resident notified the RCMP that he looked like a man who was rooming at her home. This man had said his name was Albert McAuliffe. Further inquiries in the area led to Germain Noel, who testified that Herbert McAuliffe had been renting a double garage from him for the past four years. A police search of the building turned up not only a car, but something much more significant.

The garage housed a range of machinery, including a lathe, grinder, and drill press. In addition was all the essential equipment for counterfeiting 50-cent pieces. Several samples of the finished product lay around — perfect counterfeits that could have fooled anyone — as well as thousands of unfinished pieces. It was later suggested that one reason the thief had taken the coins during the robbery was to use the silver to coat the 50-cent pieces.

This was the only recorded instance of any counterfeiter in Canada focusing on coins rather than bills, and it was obvious the suspect was brilliant with machinery.

Thanks to items from the garage, including an army identification card with fingerprints and a picture, police were at last able to positively identify the man in custody. They also found a birth certificate for one Joseph Herbert McAuliffe, born January 8, 1918, to William Edward and Mary McAuliffe. His army record listed him as Herbert Joseph McAuliffe and showed he had been a Staff Sergeant Armament Artificer — an expert on guns. He had received an honourable discharge from the army. The RCMP also found numerous weapons in the garage, most of which were army souvenirs.

Publication of the suspect's photo also led to a man making an inquiry at the North Bay detachment of the Ontario Provincial Police. He thought the person in the picture resembled his son, Herbert, whom he said he had not seen for 14 years. He was right.

Herbert McAuliffe was scheduled for a preliminary hearing in Simcoe on July 17, 1950. In the sweltering heat of a Norfolk county courtroom, 23 witnesses testified that Herbert was responsible for the bank robbery and the murders of Goddyn and Lierman. His trial was scheduled for September 1950.

Because the accused lacked funds for his own defence, the court retained a 24-year-old Simcoe lawyer, W.E. Ross, to defend him. It was Ross's first major criminal case.

In a seven-day trial, the longest up to that time in Norfolk County, the Crown presented 53 witnesses. The defence presented none. Among the witnesses for the Crown was firearms expert Andrew Mason-Rooke, who stated that the rifle found in the dead men's car had not been recently fired and could not be discharged because of dirt in the firing parts. When pushed, however, he would not say absolutely that it could not be fired or had not been.

In closing, Ross stated that because there was provocation in the double slaying, his client should be found guilty of manslaughter, not murder. Justice Treleaven, however, immediately declared that provocation as a defence was not open to the accused, and that manslaughter was not an option the jury could choose. Ross had also put forth a self-defence plea. Treleaven told the jury that if they found the bank robber to be the same man who had done the shooting and he had intended to kill or do bodily harm to anyone who got in his way, then a plea of self-defence was not acceptable either.

The jury apparently agreed and, after less than three hours, they found Herbert McAuliffe guilty of murder. He was sentenced to hang on December 19, 1950. As he left the courtroom, the convict brushed past a young woman who had been unable to get in to watch the trial. It was his sister, Irene.

Appeals were launched in an attempt to save McAullife's life. In one of them, Arthur Maloney, a lawyer now working on the prisoner's behalf, argued that the trial judge was wrong in telling the jury they could not bring in a verdict of manslaughter. All appeals were rejected. Various legions and veterans associations submitted requests for clemency, as

Herbert McAuliffe

did the McAuliffe family. It was pointed out that his child-hood had been very difficult. After their mother's funeral, the young Herbie and Irene had gone to live with their ailing grandmother. Their father then remarried, and had another son. After seven years, the children moved home with their father, who abused and mistreated Herbie.

"Herbie returned to his father and step-mother," his aunt, Mrs. Quinn, wrote in a letter to Canada's Minister of Justice two weeks before the scheduled execution. "His home life from then on was very unhappy. I visited that home on different occasions and I saw for myself that Herbie was unwanted. However, he was forced to live in that cruel atmosphere for several years. Herbie was a boy that never asked for sympathy. At times when I visited his home, he was severely reprimanded for trivial childish acts and never once did I hear him give a nasty retort.

"But this continuous nagging and fault finding bothered him and made him very unhappy. He seemed to feel alone in a world where he wasn't wanted. These circumstances drove him to leave home when he was only about sixteen."

She continued, "I am a sister of this boy's father and my heart aches for this unhappy boy. So I am pleading with you for clemency."

In a National Film Board documentary on the case, *Murder Remembered, Norfolk County 1950*, McAuliffe's young lawyer, W.E. Ross, says he had been unaware of his client's childhood. Had he known those facts, he explains, he would have handled things differently. He also describes what happened when he contacted McAuliffe's father.

"I wrote his father that I was a young and inexperienced lawyer and that his son should have the benefit of the top criminal lawyer in the province. I remember his father saying, 'I wouldn't spend a nickel on his defence.'"

Eight days before he was to be hanged, McAuliffe wrote a letter to Minister of Justice Sinclair Garson. He explained what had happened on the day of the robbery, and how hard he'd tried to get away from the men chasing him.

"No matter how fast I went I never seemed to be able to get away from them," he wrote. "After a little while I could see that one was pointing a gun at me."

He then turned down a side road, but had only driven about a hundred metres when he heard a shot close to his car. He looked back again in the mirror and could see a man leaning out the window with a rifle pointed at him.

"I heard another shot pass close by," wrote McAuliffe. "I ducked my head out of fear because I was sure he was going to hit me with a bullet. When I did this, my car was on the soft shoulder and I lost control of it and it went into the ditch."

Now the pursuing was really close, and when McAuliffe looked back, "the same man had the rifle to his shoulder, pointing it at me." McAuliffe then fired at the car randomly before jumping out of his vehicle and running over to the driver's side of his pursuers' car.

"The man with the rifle seemed to be trying to pull the rifle back into the car. I thought he was going to try and shoot again," McAuliffe's letter went on. "I was so frightened about my own life that I don't know what I really did because I lost control of myself and my own gun ... I swear to God that I never intended to kill anyone or to do anybody any harm. The only reason this happened was because I was afraid they'd kill me ..."

Herbert's sister Irene also wrote to Garson, pleading for her brother's life. She pointed to his war service. "If my brother had not been taught to shoot so effectively in the last war for his country, he would not have used a gun at all," she said. "You can't awaken in men a desire to kill in self-protection during wartime and then expect that desire to die a sudden death."

Their childhood, she also affirmed, had been a nightmare. "After my father's second marriage, we were very unhappy. Our home life as children leaves a scar on our hearts we will never forget."

All pleas fell on deaf ears. According to the film *Murder Remembered*, McAuliffe wrote in his last letter to Irene, "I'm crying for the first time, I believe, since we were kids together. Tonight I am going to die. I'm a man and I will die like a man. I love you." It was signed "Brother Herbie."

As with everything else in McAuliffe's life, the hanging at the Simcoe County Jail did not go smoothly. The doctor present at the execution said the hanging was botched, that the condemned man took 16 minutes to die because his neck did not break; he died mainly from strangulation.

The priest in attendance at the hanging was greatly affected by the incident. In *Murder Remembered* he says he had not anticipated going to the gallows with a young man and watching him die. He was, he explains, forever after disturbed by it.

"I stood at the top of the upper room and he wanted me to hold him, which I did, and then he fell."

Chapter 2
Advertisement for Murder

"CANADA. — University man — having farm —wishes to meet gentleman's son to live with him and learn the business, with view to partnership; must invest five hundred pounds to extend stock; board, lodging, and 5 per cent interest till partnership arranged."
Times, London, England, 1889

I t was a complete scam. The farm did not even exist. However, this fact was not known to one unsuspecting Englishman who answered the ad and went on a journey far longer than the one he'd anticipated.

* * *

In December 1888, Lord and Lady Somerset arrived in the Ontario town of Woodstock. A young couple in their early twenties, they became well known to everyone in the area. Lord Somerset did not have a job, but then he didn't seem to need one as he spread his spending around. He enjoyed driving his buggy, hunting, and taking his wife on picnics. One of his favourite spots was Pine Pond, which he discovered while hunting with a friend in nearby Blenheim Swamp.

In May 1889, a mere six months after appearing in Woodstock, the Somersets abruptly left. One friend in town received a note from Lord Somerset, who explained he and his wife had returned to England because a family member was dying. "I am coming out to Woodstock shortly, I hope," the letter also said. "I owe you something, I know. Please let me know, and tell Scott, the grocer, to make out his bill, and anyone else if I owe anybody anything."

The Somersets were not heard from again.

* * *

"Farm pupils" were common in Canada in 1889. These were young men from good families in England who travelled over to work and learn the skill of farming. Douglas Pelly — a "university man" — answered the ad in the *Times*. Through a broker, who acted as a go-between for the owners of the farms and interested young men, Pelly met the man who ran the ad, John Reginald Birchall. At 24, Birchall was actually a year younger than Pelly, but certainly seemed more successful. The men corresponded extensively before finally meeting in early January 1890.

"He represented that he had a business connected with horses," Pelly later recalled, "that it consisted of buying horses in the rough ... growing them up and trimming them and feeding them and selling them at a profit and that it was carried on at a farm ... about a mile and a half from [Niagara] Falls, this is on the Canadian side."

Birchall made the venture sound very attractive to his prospective farm pupil. He told Pelly his farm had "a good brick house and in regular English style ... lit with gas." He also said he had English servants, as well as farm buildings and stables lit by electric light.

Birchall relayed all the details about his business to Pelly, including the fact he had a contract with the Canadian Pacific Railway to provide horses for them on jobs. He said he had been in Canada off and on for eight years, originally coming to the country in the same capacity as Pelly planned to. In Birchall's case, he said he was able to finally buy the farm he worked on.

The two men soon reached an agreement whereby Pelly would buy 22.5 percent of the profits in the business for £170 (approximately $800).

Reg Birchall and his wife, Florence, met Pelly in London, and they travelled together to Liverpool on the evening of February 4, ready to sail the next day for New York. It was much to Pelly's surprise on the train to Liverpool when Birchall told him they were to be joined on the trip by another man, Frederick Cornwallis Benwell — the son of a Colonel Benwell, who Birchall claimed was a friend of his.

"He said young Benwell was coming out as a farm pupil and he was going to be settled on a farm," Pelly recalled. "He said he did not like him … [that] he was a rather comical sort of man and … described him as a man I would not very much care about."

As a result of these comments, Pelly initially avoided Benwell. However, the two did eventually have a conversation, and Benwell told Pelly that he was going out to live at the farm and that he expected to be Birchall's partner in time. When Pelly confronted Birchall with this, the latter responded by explaining that while Benwell might have thought that was going to happen, it wasn't.

"He expressed the opinion that Benwell was a great nuisance and he wished he had never brought him at all," Pelly said. Birchall also told Pelly that he intended to get Benwell placed on a farm as soon as possible "to get rid of him."

Onboard ship, the four passengers happened to meet I.F. Hellmuth, a lawyer from London, Ontario. Years later, in one of the articles he wrote about his career, Hellmuth observed about that encounter: "There was one matter that appeared rather curious to me at the time. Birchall was frequently in company with either Benwell or Pelly, but very rarely were the three together. I took quite a fancy to Benwell

The young Frederick Cornwallis Benwell

… a genial and attractive youngster … who spoke as though he did not entirely appreciate being shipped off by his father to the colonies."

The group arrived in New York on Friday, February 14, 1890, and stayed at the Metropolitan Hotel. While there, they bumped into someone who greeted the Birchalls with "Lord and Lady Somerset — how wonderful to see you!" When Pelly expressed surprise at this, Birchall had a ready answer.

Somerset, he explained, was the name of the man whose farm he had been a pupil on (the farm he'd eventually bought), and people thought he was the man's son.

The following night the foursome travelled up to Buffalo, where they checked into Stafford House. There, the three men discussed their plans for the next morning. It was decided that Birchall would take Benwell to his farm first, and that Pelly would stay behind with Mrs. Birchall and wait to hear from them. The reason Birchall gave for this arrangement was that he wanted to surprise the people at the farm and make sure everything was in order for the visit. He also told Pelly he would send a telegram the next day by 2:00 p.m. with further instructions.

Birchall and Benwell set off at 6:00 a.m. on February 17. Pelly stayed close to the hotel, but the hours passed and no telegram arrived. Finally, at 9:00 p.m., he received one from Birchall saying they would have to stay in Buffalo another night. Half an hour later, Birchall showed up in person.

He told Pelly he'd taken Benwell to the farm, but that the new pupil had not liked it. He'd then shown Benwell one or two other places, but the young man hadn't cared for those either. In the end he had given Benwell the names of some other farmers "up country" and had accompanied the "rather sulky" youngster either onto the train or partway to the train — Pelly later couldn't remember exactly what Birchall had said.

Birchall also shared with Pelly the fact that when he and

Benwell had arrived at the farm, "he found it had been let temporarily by his overseer to some tenants ... [They] were dirty folks and the farm was in a rather poor sort of state."

Pelly and the Birchalls departed for the town of Niagara Falls, Ontario, the next day, taking everything with them, including Benwell's belongings. They left all the baggage in Niagara Falls, New York, until they found a boarding house on the Canadian side. The following morning they returned to the American side and took everything through customs, with Birchall using a set of keys to open Benwell's bags for inspection.

A week later — a week during which Pelly still had not been taken to the farm — Birchall mentioned that Benwell had sent a telegram asking that his luggage be sent to a hotel in New York.

* * *

George and Joseph Eldridge lived in the vicinity of Blenheim Swamp and were often out hunting or chopping wood in the area. The swamp was more than two and a half kilometres long. An old hunter's trail, known to anyone living in the area, led through the swamp to Pine Pond. However, a fire in the peaty soil under the trees in May 1889 had destroyed the entrance to the trail near the road.

Late on the morning of February 21, 1890, the Eldridge brothers were out in the swamp when they stumbled on the body of a young man. The tangled mess of vegetation in the area made their discovery a little like finding a needle in a haystack. The body had obviously been there a few days and, with the rainfall and the freezing temperatures, parts of it had frozen into strange positions, caked in ice. The authorities were notified and came immediately. At first, identifying the body seemed impossible. Not only had the victim's pockets been emptied, but the personal labels sewn into his clothes had been cut off every article.

Another search the following day, however, turned up the first clues. One of the Eldridge brothers found a cigar holder with half a cigar still in it. On the spot where the body had lain the day before was a pair of eyeglasses, and more than three metres away was a brown leather cigar case that had obviously been stepped on. Handwritten in ink on the inside of the case was *F.C. Benwell*.

Detective John Wilson Murray was called in to handle the investigation. He took photos of the body and had the information about the cigar case publicized in the newspapers.

Birchall had just been out picking up the mail on February 28 when he rushed back to the boarding house and ran up to his room. A few minutes later Pelly was summoned upstairs.

"[Birchall] told me," Pelly later testified in court, "that he had seen in the paper the account of the finding of a cigar case near the body of a man who had been murdered up in this part of the world, near Woodstock ... with 'F.C. Benwell'

Dead Man's Swamp. Benwell's body was found resting partly on the tree stump in the centre of the photograph.

written on it. He said he thought we might go off at once to see the body, to see if it was Benwell or not."

They decided that Birchall and his wife would go to see if they could identify the body, and that Pelly would go to the hotel in New York where Benwell was supposedly staying. It was Birchall who also brought up the subject of his revolver.

"Do you know," he told Pelly, "that Benwell has got my pistol." He claimed that Benwell had taken it from him.

After travelling to Princeton, Ontario, and confirming that the murdered man was indeed Benwell, the Birchalls met with Detective Murray. In a memoir he wrote some years later, Murray described the couple as follows:

"The gentleman was dressed in perfect taste. He was handsome and easy in manner, with a certain grace of bearing that was quite attractive. He came toward me, and I saw he was about five feet nine inches tall, supple, clean cut, well built. His hair was dark and fashionably worn; his forehead was broad and low. He wore a light moustache. Two dark-brown eyes flashed at me in greeting. Clearly he was a man of the world, a gentleman, accustomed to the good things of life, a likeable chap, who had lived well and seen much and enjoyed it in his less than thirty years on earth. The lady stood by the window looking out. She was a slender, pleasant-faced blonde, a bit weary about the eyes, but evidently a woman of refinement."

It did not take long for suspicion about who murdered Benwell to fall on Reg Birchall. I.F. Hellmuth, the lawyer the group had met on the ship en route to New York, received a telegram from Pelly that said simply, "BIRCHALL ARRESTED WANTS YOU TO COME DOWN AT ONCE." Hellmuth thought the arrest might be related to some minor prank and sent a telegram back to Pelly asking about the charge. He was astonished to receive the reply, "CHARGE IS MURDER OF BENWELL."

When arrested, Birchall was found to have Benwell's keys in his pocket. He also had in his possession a special pencil case that Benwell had always carried, inscribed for his 13th birthday. Florence Birchall was also arrested as an accessory after the fact, although the charges against her were shortly dropped.

The trial, which took place between September 21 and 29 in the Old Town Hall in Woodstock, attracted worldwide attention from the start. More than 50 journalists showed up from across Canada and the United States to cover the proceedings, and even the *Times* (London) sent its own reporters. Tickets were sold for admission to the courtroom.

Hellmuth realized immediately that the only way his client stood a chance of acquittal was if they hired a lawyer with much more experience than Hellmuth himself had. George Blackstock was retained and became senior counsel. As he did in so many other important criminal cases in Ontario, Bath "Brick" Osler led the prosecution.

Birchall, who cut such a dashing figure that women sent him flowers and other gifts, continually stated that the Crown would never be able to pin the murder on him. He said there was no proof that he and Benwell had gotten off the train at Eastwood, the only station near the location of the murder. However, in very short order, Osler produced witness after witness to demonstrate that Birchall was a liar. He showed that while Birchall had been working out a deal with Pelly, he'd also been courting young Benwell through his father, Colonel Benwell. Benwell senior had not been as gullible as Pelly, though, and would not agree to a deal for his son without there first being a trip to Canada to see the farm. He'd said that if the visit went well, then he would give Birchall £500 (approximately $2500) for a 50 percent stake in the business.

The accused's defence was quickly crumbling. Birchall's lawyers did not even attempt to come up with an alibi for their client, and they could not risk putting him on the stand in light of his previous trip to Canada under the alias of Lord Somerset.

Finally, the Crown introduced the most damning piece of evidence in the case: a letter Birchall had written to Colonel Benwell on February 20, 1890. "My Dear Sir," it began. "We arrived safely here after a very pleasant journey, the sea being rather rough than otherwise." Then it went on:

Your son has inspected all my books and all my business arrangements, and I introduced him to people who know me well. He suggested taking other advice so I of course was perfectly willing and he consulted a barrister in London, Ontario, concerning the business, with satisfactory results: and he has decided to join me as he found all that he wished to be satisfactory. I think we shall make a very good business together. The books show a very good profit for last year. I think the best way is to place the money in our joint names in the bank to the credit of our reserve fund ... We are holding a large sale early in March, and your son was somewhat anxious to share in the profits of the sale which I am quite willing that he should do and so we have signed our deed of partnership and

*shall, I am sure, never regret doing so. Your son is, I
think, writing to you by this post …*

*I think you will be pleased that your son has
found things satisfactory and I quite agree that he did
the best thing in coming out to see the business first. I
shall send you weekly particulars of all business done
so that you can see for yourself how things go on …*

*We have opened a business account in our joint
names at the American bank here. Your son will
doubtless explain his views in his letter.*

More than any other bit of evidence, the letter clearly
showed Birchall's scheming ways and established a motive for
the murder. Because it had been written three days after the
murder, it effectively tightened the noose around Birchall's
neck. Even he knew he had made a big mistake. Once, in the
weeks leading up to his death, he was professing his innocence to someone who reminded him about the letter.

"I was a damned fool to write that letter," he replied.

The guilty verdict was no surprise. John Reginald
Birchall was sentenced to hang on November 14, 1890.

Just as Birchall never stopped professing his innocence,
he also never stopped trying to make a buck and doing what
he could to ensure his name would not soon be forgotten. He
wrote a book (essentially an autobiography — large on colour
but short on truth) and negotiated with a number of big-city
newspapers to publish it, hoping to acquire some money

for his wife, who had remained steadfastly by his side. Titled *A Swamp of Death*, the book did not include a confession. He eventually received, it was reported, $2500 for the manuscript.

As had occurred from the beginning, Birchall continued to elicit a morbid curiosity from the public at large. People were relentless in attempting to see him or obtain something belonging to him.

Birchall himself commented on this, writing in his book, "It is indeed strange to notice how people will go out of their way to catch a glimpse of an unsavoury prisoner ... [but] not go out of their way even to hear their clergyman preach or to see anything that may improve their minds."

But this observation didn't stop them. Folk songs were written about him. People frequently sent him letters at the prison in the hopes of getting a reply so they would have his autograph. Even Birchall's hangman got into the act. He made sure the rope was an extra 10 feet long, and after the hanging he sold pieces by the inch.

One of the oddest transactions, however, was made by Wonderland, a wax museum scheduled to open on Toronto's Yonge Street around the time of the execution. Wonderland purchased the outfit Birchall had been wearing on the day of the murder, and had a contract that allowed them to exhibit a wax head, bust, and figure of him. They paid $150 for the privilege. Florence Birchall delivered the outfit the day before her husband's execution. In the pocket happened to be a

receipt dated February 4, 1890 — the day before the foursome had left Liverpool for New York. Among the items listed
on the receipt was the revolver used to kill Benwell.

During the hanging, Birchall's neck did not break and it
took him six and a half minutes to die. Even in death, though,
he couldn't resist one last parting shot. On the day of his execution, the following statement ("all rights reserved")
appeared in the Woodstock *Sentinel-Review*:

> *Woodstock Gaol, Nov. 10, 1890*
> *If after my death there shall appear in the press,
> or in any other manner whatsoever, any confession
> that I had any hand in the murder of Mr. F.C. Benwell
> or any previous knowledge of said murder, with intent
> or malice aforethought, or any personal connection
> with the murder on the 17th February, or other day, or
> any knowledge that any such murder was likely to be
> committed, or any statement further than any I may
> have made previous to this date ... any confession or
> partial confession are entirely fictitious and in no way
> were written by me, neither emanated from me in any
> way whatsoever to any person, and the whole are ficti-
> tious and without a word of truth. This likewise
> applies to my story in* The Mail *in which I have made
> no such confession or partial confession ...*

It was signed "Reg Birchall."

Reverend Wade — the minister who stayed by Birchall's side for most of the condemned man's last 24 hours — did not see this statement until after the execution. When it was brought to his notice, he was very upset. Before heading to the burial service at 5 p.m., he told John Markey, chief reporter for the *Sentinel-Review*, that the latter should join him at the jail where, Wade said with some passion, "I want to deny that terrible lie which you published this morning in Birchall's statement!"

During the burial ceremony, Wade refused to read the Episcopal service, instead simply intoning a passage of Scripture and saying a short prayer that read in part: "Man has done his best and the law has done its worse and now the body of this poor, deluded sinful man we confide to the earth."

* * *

Many years later, I.F. Hellmuth wrote a series of stories for *Maclean's* about his more famous cases, the Birchall one being at the top of the list. Hellmuth called Reg Birchall "the coolest customer I ever encountered, absolutely without fear but also without a vestige of gratitude for any help or assistance he received."

Hellmuth also disclosed that during the trial, prosecutor Brick Osler had repeatedly read Birchall's letter to Colonel Benwell aloud, asking the jury what they could hear between the lines. Finally he'd answered his own question, "shouting 'Murder! Murder! Murder' until the whole courtroom rang with the words."

Some months after Birchall's execution, Hellmuth had found himself sitting next to Osler on a train, "when [Osler] suddenly turned to [him] and asked what [he] thought of his attitude in the Birchall case." Hellmuth had replied that he thought Osler had conducted the case "in a vindictive spirit." His assessment, it turned out, was an accurate one.

Osler had gone on to tell Hellmuth that he'd travelled to England shortly before the trial and had found a widow who'd answered Birchall's ad on behalf of her only son. When Birchall had told the widow and her son that the fee was £500, the woman had said it was way beyond her means to pay, and no deal had been made. Not long after that, however, she'd received a letter from the man telling her that if she gave him 100 pounds and insured her son's life in Birchall's favour, he (Birchall) would take the young man to Canada.

Osler had been so angry when he saw this letter, said Hellmuth, that he'd "felt he had to deal with a reptile and ... was determined to crush Birchall."

And in the end he did.

Chapter 3
'Til Death Do Us Part

"I, George Sternaman, having had very peculiar
attacks at times during the past six months, and of
which no one but my wife and a few of her relatives
know anything of, write this letter to state that
if I should die whilst in one of them that no person
can say that it was by her hands in any way that I died.
The only cause or reason of my having these is when
I get downhearted or worrying about anything
that does not go to please me."
Buffalo, New York, June 10, 1896

S o read part of a "To Whom It May Concern"
declaration written by Olive Sternaman's
husband, George. He concluded in it, "I
hope what I have written will convince all that they may not
think that my wife had anything to do with such an uncom-
mon death."

In spite of his plea, Olive would be suspected when George died on August 19, 1896, in Rainham Township, Ontario. Six days prior to his death, she had brought the very sick man from Buffalo to the home of his mother in Ontario.

And Buffalo is where the story began.

* * *

Olive Adele Sevenpiper was born in 1867 and spent her early years in Sweet's Corners, South Cayuga, Ontario. When she was 12, her family moved to Buffalo, where it wasn't long before she found a job doing general housework. It was in Buffalo that she met her husband to be, Ezra Chipman.

Ezra was a skilled carpenter who had moved to the U.S. from St. Catharines, Ontario, to make more money. By all accounts he was a hard-working, affable man. He and Olive married in February 1886 and moved into a comfortable home in Black Rock, now part of Buffalo but once notorious as the starting point of a Fenian raid into Canada. Two sons were born to the couple, one in 1887 and the other in 1889, and the family lived a happy existence.

In 1893, Ezra met a young man working on a construction site not far from their Black Rock home. Like Ezra, 20-year-old George Sternaman was a hard worker who had moved to Buffalo from Ontario the previous year in search of work. Ezra took George under his wing, and one night in 1894, he told Olive that George needed a place to stay until his current job was finished. He said the young Canadian would be coming by in the morning to arrange board for a few weeks.

"Sternaman came, and after the job was finished he did not say anything about leaving," Olive later recalled. "My husband and I talked it over and decided he could stay if he wished. My husband and Sternaman often worked together … we were all friendly."

So friendly, in fact, that the Chipmans and George took a holiday together back to Ontario in 1894, to the Rainham agricultural fair. They visited with Olive's friends and family and even with George's mother, Eliza Sternaman. It seemed Eliza took an instant dislike to Olive, perhaps because she could sense the obvious feelings her son was harbouring for his landlady.

Olive and Ezra were oblivious to young George's feelings, but Olive's sister Lizzie and her mother weren't. At one point during the visit, Olive fell dangerously ill, and a doctor told the family she was going to die. Upon hearing this news from Lizzie, George began to sob uncontrollably and then started vomiting. It took him almost as long to recover as it did Olive, who (contrary to the doctor's diagnosis) did not die.

Later that year, George returned to Ontario for a second time. His father was dying from cancer, and George went home to be with him. Shortly after he passed away, George discovered his father had a life insurance policy. So impressed was George with the benefits to his family that he took out a policy on his own life, making his mother the beneficiary. By the beginning of October 1894, George was back in Buffalo, and back under the Chipmans' roof.

That same fall, Ezra began to complain of being constantly exhausted. Still, he managed to carry on working — at least until Christmas Eve day. That morning, Ezra and George headed off to their respective jobs, each carrying the lunches Olive had packed for them. During their break, Ezra and his boss, William Randall, went up to the attic at the job site, where Randall used an oil stove to warm their meal.

"He seemed all right forenoon," Randall later said of Ezra. "He was sitting by the stairway and he eat his dinner until he come to his pie. He ate about two thirds of the pie and threw the rest of it over in the corner, in a pile of wood cutting that we had."

"Gad," Ezra apparently muttered, "I guess the old woman got cayenne pepper in her pie this time instead of spice." Before long, Ezra was vomiting and unable to keep working. He asked to go home.

"He said his stomach burned so that he couldn't hardly stand the pain," Randall recalled.

Ezra's pain worsened over the following weeks, and Olive finally sent for their family doctor. Despite the doctor's urgings, she would not hear of Ezra going to a hospital. Another doctor was consulted on January 19, 1895, but he also had no luck in persuading the Chipmans to have Ezra admitted to a hospital. Both doctors, however, had drawn the same conclusion: Ezra was likely suffering from a type of metallic poisoning, probably arsenic.

Soon after the doctors' visit, Ezra died. Despite having some reservations, the family doctor signed the death certificate, stating death was due to multiple neuritis (inflammation of the nerves) and paralysis.

During the period of Ezra's decline, George had taken up the slack in helping around the house and contributing much-needed money to the household finances. And then, even after Ezra's death, he continued to board with Olive. Although it was common practice in those days for women to run boarding houses — a typical way for widows and single women to make money — the gossip about this arrangement ran rampant: Olive's husband had died mysteriously (poisoned by his wife, perhaps?) and she was now living in the same house with another man.

In February 1895, Eliza Sternaman came to visit George, and she heard the rumours. Not liking Olive to begin with, she became convinced the gossip was true and that Olive *had* poisoned her husband. George was upset that his mother would think such a thing, and she soon went back to Canada.

That September, Olive and George attended the Rainham fair again. When Olive returned to Buffalo, George stayed behind for a visit and told his mother he was thinking of marrying Olive. (Olive later reported that George had proposed to her in July.) Eliza was angry at the thought of their marriage and tried everything to persuade George to change his mind, pointing out their age difference (Olive was 29 and George was 22 at the time) and the fact that she already had children. But of particular concern to Eliza was the possibility that the rumours were true — that Olive had poisoned Ezra for the insurance money and that she was now after George's insurance policies as well.

It's not known whether Eliza was really worried for George or for her own vested interest in his policies, which were then in her name. However, she did warn George that if he married Olive he'd be dead in six months.

That prediction was almost dead on.

In letters to her, George tried to win his mother over to the idea of his marrying Olive. "I always tried to do the best I could for you," he wrote to Eliza, but said she was asking too much in wanting him "to give up the one I love."

"I think that you had not ought to think so hard of her because you have no proof for what you have heard," he also noted to his mother, and then told her his mind was made up.

George married Olive on February 3, 1896 (coincidentally, 10 years to the day that Ezra and Olive were married), and his new wife became the beneficiary of the insurance policies.

Little known to that point was that George had some serious emotional problems and suffered from what he called "spells." Sometimes, during these, he would sit still for hours as if in a trance. Other times he became very agitated, suffering what was later described in a summation of the trial to come as "a species of attack somewhat hysterical in character, due to jealousy, or coming on when he was worried or annoyed."

George never consulted a doctor about these spells, which seemed to disappear once he and Olive were married. The marriage seemed, for the most part, a happy one, although George was known to be very possessive of his new wife. He had also flown into a few rages over the photograph of Ezra that she insisted on displaying.

In April 1896, George applied to the Metropolitan Life Insurance Company for a $1000 policy on his life. Dr. William Langley, an agent of the company, examined him and found his physical condition to be good. And, when Langley was filling in the application form and asked, "Have you ever had any fits or convulsions?" George answered, "No." He was deemed to be "a thoroughly good risk," and his application for insurance was approved.

At work one day in early June, George suddenly became very sick. After eating the berries in his lunch, he started vomiting and felt a burning sensation in his mouth, throat, and stomach. Olive hovered over him for a week because his symptoms mimicked those Ezra had suffered from the previous year. After a few days, George recovered, but he grew increasingly moody. Then, on June 9, he had one of his spells, something he had not experienced for months. Olive's sister Lizzie witnessed it.

Olive encouraged George to write to his mother and tell her about these spells, but he was reluctant to do so.

Although the couple tried to ignore them, Olive and George were not completely unaware of the rumours surrounding the death of Ezra. On June 10, in an effort to protect his wife, George wrote his strange declaration, "To Whom It May Concern." In it, he admitted to having the spells and absolved Olive of any responsibility were he to die while in the midst of one. He also wrote that he had not gone to a doctor about the spells "because I always come out of them all right."

On June 13, 1896, after eating his lunch (which again included berries), George once more began vomiting violently and had to go home. Olive called in Dr. Edward Frost, who treated George for a gastric illness and then returned the next day to check on him. Of the illness George had experienced in early June, Frost later recalled that his patient had "complained of a sweetish taste in his mouth and general lassitude. Said he simply did not feel well."

George continued to deteriorate, developing backache, genital sores, and swelling in the groin. Frost said that, "he had the appearance of a man suffering from toxemia; that is a man who was being poisoned by some underlying disease." Frost tried treating the patient with minute doses of arsenic — commonly used in those days to treat a number of illnesses, including chronic diarrhea and gastric ulcers — but he discontinued this prescription when George did not improve. Frost also examined for, and then dismissed, the possibility of syphilis.

49

By July 4, George had numerous sores in his mouth, increasing weakness, and swollen glands. The mucous membranes of his eyes and nose were also irritated. A week later, he was complaining "of a tingling, numbness, in the fingers and also in the lower extremities."

Frost started to suspect his patient was showing signs of arsenic poisoning — not from the brief treatment the doctor had prescribed, but from some other source. He brought in another physician, Dr. William Phelps, who agreed with Frost's assessment. Together they tried to persuade the Sternamans to put George in the hospital. In this the doctors were unsuccessful.

"At that time after [Olive] had objected so strongly, I told her that I understood that she had had one husband die under suspicious circumstances and asked her what she thought people would think if another husband died under similar circumstances," Frost later said. "She remarked, 'Doctor, if he dies I will have an autopsy and that will clear me.'"

Soon after this discussion, Eliza Sternaman arrived in Buffalo to see her ailing son. She was not happy with Dr. Frost and insisted on a new doctor. Frost then took Olive aside to talk to her. "I said: 'I will say to you now something which I have not said before, and that is that your husband has had marked symptoms of poisoning and of poisoning by arsenic, but, understand, that all of these symptoms may be explained by disease. I also said, 'If this becomes public, it becomes so through you and not through me.'"

Frost also stated later that Olive told him about an incident that had occurred during a spell George had suffered before the onset of his illness. Frustrated by George's severely depressed and catatonic behaviour, she had bemoaned aloud the state of her marriage and wondered what Ezra would think if he knew she had come to this. Hearing her say this, George had become very despondent and suicidal.

Eliza Sternaman brought in a Dr. Saltsman, who diagnosed a chronic atrophy of the liver and multiple neuritis. By this time, George was bedridden, unable to move his arms or legs. He could not keep any water down, and was forced to lie with a piece of wet muslin between his lips to keep his mouth moist. Under Dr. Saltsman's care, however, George's condition turned around considerably. Before long, Eliza returned to Canada; her son was once again moving about, able to eat, and regaining his strength. As a result of this improvement, Saltsman stopped seeing him on August 10.

Within a day, George's condition deteriorated rapidly.

When Olive wrote to her mother-in-law asking her to come back to Buffalo because she needed help, Eliza said she couldn't, but suggested they come to her. Since the family's funds were severely depleted, Olive, George, and the two boys decided that was the best plan. They reached Cayuga on August 12 and travelled by wagon to Rainham Township. Saltsman had warned against the journey, so Olive asked Eliza to arrange for a doctor to be there on the evening they arrived to reassure her no harm had been done. Eliza did not do this, so it wasn't until the next day that Dr. Philip Park saw George.

Park found a very sick man. In addition to having a pulse rate of 120, George was constipated, emaciated, and without a voice. The inside of his mouth was covered in white patches and ulcers, and his skin was dark in colour and peeling off all over his body. On top of all that, the man was suffering from partial paralysis and in terrible pain. The symptom he complained of most was a burning in the soles of his feet.

Almost immediately, Park felt sure he was dealing with arsenic poisoning. He was therefore surprised when tests of a urine sample from his patient showed no arsenic at all. He didn't tell the family what he thought, but asked for another doctor to assist him. On August 16, a Dr. Harrison was called in and quickly agreed with Park. They decided to keep a close eye on the situation.

"From the history of the case ... we felt certain that no arsenic had been administered to him for several weeks before he left Buffalo," Harrison later stated. "We felt certain also from what we saw at that time that no arsenic had been administered to him in Rainham while he was under our charge and especially from the fact Dr. Park had examined the urine and found nothing present."

On Monday, August 17, with George now weaker than ever, Park warned the family that the sick man did not have long to live. He was right. On Tuesday evening, George had another attack of vomiting, and by the early hours of

Wednesday, August 19, he was dead. The day of George's death, Eliza asked Olive how much insurance George had on his life. She was told $770.

Dr. Park asked Olive that day if her husband had any enemies in Buffalo because, he told her, the symptoms might easily be accounted for by poison. "What kind of poison?" she asked him. Park answered by asking her if he was the first doctor to raise the possibility of poisoning. She replied that he was.

True to her word, Olive asked for a post mortem. Doctors Park and Harrison performed the autopsy and Harrison took some of the body fluid to do more tests for arsenic. He did not find any. George was buried and, that same day, Olive and her boys left for Buffalo and moved in with Ezra Chipman's mother.

In September, Olive received a letter from Eliza. Because Olive had insurance, Eliza felt entitled to ask her for $25 as compensation for feeding the family in the last week of George's life and to cover the errands George's brothers had run. Olive ignored the request. About the same time, Eliza discovered there was another policy on George's life. Whether her next actions were because of this discovery or because Olive did not give her $25 is unknown. Whatever the reason, she went to see Haldimand County's Crown attorney, C.W. Coulter, and told him her suspicions. Coulter then contacted coroner David Thompson, who immediately called an inquest.

George had not been lying in peace for long when his body was exhumed. Park and Harrison performed a second autopsy and shipped several organs off for testing. The corpse, six weeks old by now, was well preserved — a fact that surprised the doctors because they could find no evidence of embalming. When the tests came back, they showed the presence of arsenic in George's organs.

This time, the spotlight really did focus on the deceased's widow.

On October 27, 1896, Olive was taken into custody in Buffalo and an extradition hearing was scheduled. She was sure she would be acquitted, but on the morning of December 4, she found out otherwise. Although she decided it best to return to Canada as quickly as possible, her family, friends, and lawyers in Buffalo persuaded her to fight the extradition. Sentiment, they said, would be very much against her back in the Haldimand County Courthouse in Cayuga. She battled long and hard to avoid being extradited, but in August 1897 she was escorted back to Cayuga, and to jail.

Her trial began on November 17, more than a year after George's death. Olive was defended by William German. Prosecuting for the Crown was Brick Osler, considered one of the best criminal lawyers in the country. (As was the case in those days, the top lawyers in the country were usually chosen by the prosecution to look out for the Crown's interests.)

Most of the information surrounding the murder had been covered in the papers during the extradition hearing. Eliza Sternaman also gave interviews to the *Globe and Mail* and other newspapers explaining her belief in Olive's guilt.

Most of the testimony in the three-day trial focused on medical evidence and the insurance policies. Olive didn't mention the $1000 policy because, as she later said when the question came up again, she had not made any payments on it in some time and assumed it had lapsed. Insurance was pointed to as the key motive in her trial. The prosecution also focused on the fact that George was her second husband to die under similar circumstances. They believed Ezra Chipman was murdered so that Olive could get the insurance money and marry George. The prosecution attempted to show that in both cases, Olive had encouraged the men to get life insurance — and had then killed them.

Although she took the stand in the extradition hearing, Olive did not testify at the murder trial. German decided to aim his efforts at trying to convince the court that the cause of death had not been arsenic poisoning. He failed miserably in this, although his closing arguments included a number of valid points: Why would Olive kill Ezra in the first place when he was a good provider and loving partner? And if she killed him for insurance money, why kill him so soon, when the policies contained clauses that considerably reduced the amounts if he died within the first year? German also pointed out that George had had a much stronger motive to kill Ezra than Olive had: he loved her and wanted to marry her.

The prosecution, meanwhile, made much of the fact that George had had another attack of vomiting on the last night of his life, the implication being that Olive had given him one final dose of arsenic. However, no proof could be found that Olive had purchased, or had been in possession of, arsenic.

As a counterattack against the suggestion that Olive had killed both husbands for insurance money, Ezra Chipman's mother testified on behalf of her former daughter-in-law. When asked whose idea it had been to get insurance, she said that Ezra had done it at her insistence, and that Olive had actually been opposed to it.

Four hours after Judge Armour made his charge to the jury, they returned to the court and asked if they could recommend mercy. When the judge told them they could, they delivered their verdict: guilty, with a recommendation for mercy. Olive rose and looked at the judge.

"I am not guilty," she declared. "In the eyes of God I will have a new trial and be acquitted."

Judge Armour looked directly at her and sentenced her to hang on January 20, 1898.

"Oh, oh, Judge, is that all the justice there is in this country?" she asked.

Ten of the twelve members of the jury were extremely upset because they assumed their recommendation for mercy meant Olive would not hang. They had not understood that the judge did not, in fact, have the authority to spare her life. He was required by law to sentence her to death. The jurors quickly signed declarations stating they would not have convicted her had they known she would be hanged, and they recommended that her sentence be commuted to life.

Petitions sprang up immediately. German launched appeals, but lost them all. Then Wallace Thayer, Olive's lawyer in Buffalo, got involved. First he wrote a letter to the *Globe and Mail* pleading her case. He described Olive as being the most spiritual and religious person he had ever met, and said it was her quiet faith that kept her calm and always believing things would turn in her favour. Next, Thayer wrote two letters to David Mills, Ontario's Minister of Justice. In the first one, dated January 4, 1898, he declared, "I am an attorney at law, but I did not take her case, nor do I plead her cause now as an attorney, but merely as a man seeking to prevent injustice."

Thayer pointed out that, according to Section 748 of Canada's Criminal Code, if the Minister of Justice had any reason to doubt that a person was rightfully convicted of a crime, he or she had the authority to order a new trial. "It is under this section that I address you," Thayer continued. "[The] terrible speed at which the case was rushed through and the judge's most biased summing up against the prisoner, struck me so strongly that I cannot see how anyone could regard it as a fair trial ... I trust you will believe me sincere and that my words may have some weight to prevent this monstrous wrong. Imprisonment for life is as bad as hanging; what I beg is, that the prisoner be granted a new trial."

On receiving an encouraging reply, Thayer's second letter to Minister of Justice Mills was sent a week before the scheduled hanging. In that letter, he criticized German's approach for the defence, saying he felt Olive should have testified on her own behalf. He also said he was convinced that George Sternaman had murdered Ezra Chipman because he'd wanted Olive for himself, and that George had then — near the beginning of his illness — decided to commit suicide by taking doses of arsenic. Had he taken even one large dose of arsenic to begin with, it would still have been enough to kill him weeks later. He wouldn't have needed to take another drop; the damage would have been done whether arsenic was still present in his system or not. Thayer maintained that any arsenic found in the body at the second autopsy would have been the result of embalming, which he believed had taken place.

His letters had a positive effect. With just over a day until Olive's execution, the sheriff of the County of Haldimand, Cayuga, Ontario, received the following telegraph:

"Minister of Justice has directed a new trial in the case of Mrs. Sternaman. You will take no further action. Answer this telegram showing you understand this message. R.W. Scott."

A reply was sent: "Message re Mrs. Sternaman received last night at 11 o'clock and clearly understood. All preparations for execution stopped. Many thanks. Robert Davis, Sheriff."

What the Minister of Justice had done was precedent setting; it was the first time the new clause in the Criminal Code had been used. Mills directed that a new trial be set for Olive, to begin on May 3, 1898.

Some people were unhappy with this turn of events, and Nicholas Davin, a Member of Parliament, introduced a bill calling for an amendment to the Criminal Code, including the repeal of Section 748. It did not succeed.

There was also a campaign to raise funds to obtain a good lawyer for Olive's defence. The government, social critics said, could afford to choose the best lawyers to defend the Crown's position, but poor clients had to rely on charity. This campaign *did* succeed.

When the second trial opened in May 1898, Osler again represented the Crown's interests. Olive's new attorney was Ebenezer Johnston, a prominent Toronto criminal lawyer who had gone up against Osler many times in the past.

While much of the second trial was a copy of the first, a big difference lay with Johnston, who was able to examine witnesses in such a way that they almost forgot their own names. For example, under his cross-examination, Eliza Sternaman admitted she had never seen anything but complete devotion from Olive towards her son. As well, she admitted that, in spite of her suspicions regarding poison, she had never attempted to remove George from Olive's care. Significantly, Johnston also got Eliza to reveal that she had started the whole murder investigation only after Olive didn't reply to her letter asking for $25.

Dr. Frost took the stand and acknowledged that George was an emotional and neurotic individual. As well, in response to Johnston's questions, he stated that Olive probably objected to George's hospitalization because it would have been a long walk for her and her two sons to get to the hospital to visit him.

One of Johnston's greatest victories, however, came in his examination of the undertaker, John Snider. Snider had insisted at the first trial that he had not embalmed the body — thereby eliminating the possibility that the arsenic found in the second autopsy had come from this source. But in the second trial, Olive's sister Lizzie swore that Snider had not only told her he'd embalmed the body, but that he'd charged the family for it. Johnston twisted Snider around so successfully that he finally admitted he dealt with so many bodies, he actually had no memory of what he did, or didn't do, in George Sternaman's case.

Dr. Thompson, coroner at the inquest, testified that he had found close to three litres of fluid in the "thoracic cavity of the body" which could have been embalming fluid. Because he had not testified to this previously, it raised doubts about the source of the arsenic found in the second autopsy.

And Johnston vigorously made a case for his belief that George had killed Ezra, and that his own illness and death were a result of a self-administered dose of arsenic. As Johnston pointed out, since Olive knew George did not have long to live, why would she have given him a final dose of arsenic on that last night to induce vomiting?

"Twice for her life. Twice within the shadow of the gallows and death," Johnston said in his four-hour address to the jury. "I want no verdict of sympathy. I want a verdict of truth and justice. Though this woman be the guiltiest alive, I maintain that the Crown has not brought it home to her."

The jury was sent out at 5:15 p.m. on May 7, 1898. Two hours later they returned to the courtroom to tell the judge they could not agree. It was later written in the newspapers that the jury was nine to three in favour of acquittal at that moment. The judge told them they had to come to a decision and sent them back to deliberate. At 9:30 p.m. they finally reached a verdict of "not guilty."

According to the *Globe and Mail,* "The great crowd of spectators sent up a shout of exhilaration which continued for fully three minutes, and which the Sheriff and his men were utterly powerless to silence. The prisoner, who had risen to her feet as soon as the words were pronounced, flushed a deep red and laughed half hysterically, while the tears rolled down her cheeks."

Olive Sternaman was finally free. After two weeks with her family and friends in Ontario, she returned to Buffalo to live with Ezra's sister. Barely five months after her acquittal, she married Frank Creutzberg of Buffalo. The relationship didn't last long. On April 12, 1900, Olive was granted a divorce from him on the grounds that he was still married to someone else. Naturally, the divorce gave rise to new rumours. It was said that one day when Frank had an attack of cramps, he accused Olive of trying to poison him. He told her if he was ever sick again he would kill her. She apparently decided not to risk it and divorced him. It made for a good story.

Her battle with Metropolitan Life for the $1000 was a long, drawn-out affair, mostly continued on her lawyers' wishes. Finally, in 1905, Olive won the money plus interest and costs. It all went to the lawyers.

Olive Adele Sevenpiper Chipman Sternaman Creutzberg never did marry again, and lived a long life, dying in 1941 at the age of 74.

Chapter 4
If Looks Could Kill

he five youngsters, ranging in age from 8 to 12, often had adventures together, but nothing prepared them for the one they became part of on a fateful Saturday in March 1946.

As the group made its way along Mountain Brow Road towards Albion Falls, just outside of Hamilton, Jimmie and Robert Weaver began squabbling. After being punched in the nose by his brother, Robert ran off down a hill. Fred Reed followed. In minutes they were racing back and screaming in panic to the other children that they had found something — a headless pig … or… part of a dead man.

After they'd all had a look at the gruesome find, the children scrambled up to the road to get help. When cars they hailed wouldn't stop, they formed a barricade across the road. Finally a vehicle pulled over. Hearing the kids' story, the couple in the car were at first skeptical, but eventually the man went down the hill to see for himself. What he saw was a male torso.

At 10:40 a.m., two officers of the Ontario Provincial Police, Leonard Mattick and Carl Farrow, arrived at the scene and began the unsavoury inspection.

Lying front down, the torso was clad only in long under-wear, the arms and legs of the garment torn away. Little blood drained from the stumps or was evident on the ground around the body. The largest amount of blood visible on the underwear, Mattick later reported, was around the neck.

When the undertaker arrived, the officers helped him turn what remained of the victim over and they saw a great deal of blood on the front of the underwear, the result of a large cut across the stomach. They also saw what they believed to be two bullet holes entering the right breast. The body was transported to Hamilton General Hospital for a closer examination to determine who the victim might be.

The autopsy took place on Monday, March 18, and was performed by the aptly named Dr. William Deadman, the pathologist at the Hamilton General Hospital. Detectives Charles Wood and Clarence Preston were in attendance.

Deadman concluded that the remains were those of a 40- to 45-year-old man, about 5 feet 10 inches tall and 185 pounds, with good muscular development. Based on the state of the body on the day of the autopsy, Deadman estimated death to have occurred between 10 to 14 days earlier. "The neck had been severed just at the level of the voice box or larynx," the pathologist reported. "The lacerations of the flesh of the neck had the appearance of having been made with a saw rather than with a keen cutting instrument."

He added that the arms and legs had also been crudely cut off with a saw and there were numerous abrasions on different parts of the body. "Across the belly, about three inches above the belly-button, was a transverse cut twelve and a half inches ... and this cut had gone through the whole belly wall for the central nine inches of its length, and underneath it were three perforations of the bowel. That cut also had the appearance of having been caused by a saw."

Regarding the gunshot wounds, Deadman drew the following conclusions: "In the central part of the right chest and in a line about one inch above the right nipple, there are two gunshot wounds three and a half inches apart," he said. "The more central one appears to be a wound of entry. The track of the bullet can be traced through the flesh to the outer wound in the flank. The ribs are not injured and the chest is not penetrated."

The wounds, he said, were caused by a .32 calibre bullet. The wound in the right side of the chest was superficial and would not have caused death.

And finally, added Deadman, a urine alcohol test revealed that the victim had been intoxicated at the time of death.

When information about the torso surfaced in the media, two city employees came forward to say that on March 7 they had found a bloody shirt on a country road and had thrown it to one side. The workers took police to the spot, and officers recovered a blood-soaked blue pinstriped shirt, its arms cut off.

The identity of the victim was still unknown, but that would change on March 19. A woman named Evelyn Dick had been phoning around to different relatives of her estranged husband, John, trying to track him down. The story she told each one was a little different every time, but the theme was the same: John owed money, people were trying to find him, and she had no idea where he was.

One such call was to the missing man's brother-in-law, John Wall. Concerned by the conversation, Wall phoned John Dick's cousin, Alex Kammerer, with whom Dick had been staying since his separation from Evelyn. Kammerer confirmed that Dick had been missing since March 6. Moreover, he told Wall, he had called the police that very afternoon when he'd heard about the torso being found. Upon giving them a description of Dick, Kammerer had been told that the body might be that of the missing man.

The following morning, Dick's relatives went together to the police station and Wall made a positive identification.

* * *

John Dick was born in Russia in 1906 and came to Canada with his family in 1924. (At some point after their move, the family changed the spelling of their name from Dyck to Dick.) As a young man, John ended up working as a motorman for the Hamilton Street Railway. Also working there was Donald MacLean, Evelyn's father.

MacLean had started working for the company as a conductor, but eventually attained a higher position — one that gave him access to company revenues. Secretly, he began to take advantage of that, and the family benefited. Evelyn's mother, Alexandra, was a dominating figure in the home. The relationship she had with her husband — a heavy drinker — was a volatile one, and the two separated often throughout their marriage.

Alexandra's wish to move in higher social circles was a desire she passed on to her daughter, who was very spoiled and always had money to throw around. Although Evelyn did not have many friends, men started noticing her by the time she was 13. From an early age she was very beautiful, and she used this to her advantage whenever she could. Hoping to help her meet the "right" people, Alexandra enrolled her daughter in the prestigious Loretto Academy. It was a very expensive school, but by dipping into the company funds Donald MacLean was able to pay for it. The family told everyone a rich aunt in Scotland was footing the bills.

Evelyn did indeed succeed in becoming well known in high society, but not in the way her mother would have liked.

Evelyn Dick in her fake Red Cross driver's uniform

Her list of high-profile boyfriends and lovers was extensive.

From an early age, lying came easily to her. Everything she did was a performance, a role she played to create an illusion or a story she made up to paint herself in a brighter glow. For example, she must have believed it would do her good to have people think she was a driver with the Red Cross in Hamilton. Obtaining the cap, jacket, and khaki skirt of a Red Cross worker (onto which she sewed phony insignia and her name), Evelyn then had her photograph taken in the full attire.

Evelyn got together with John Dick when she was 25 and he was 40. No one is quite sure why she chose to marry this penniless, older man when many richer suitors were courting her. It might have been that she was looking for some respectability: she did, after all, have a three-year-old daughter named Heather who had no apparent father. As for Dick, it seemed that he wanted to marry Evelyn because he believed she was loaded with money. The couple married on October 4, 1945. Both were to be quickly disappointed in their expectations.

On the night of the wedding, Evelyn went back to the apartment she shared with Heather and her mother (now separated from her husband). She told Dick they would have to find a larger place before they could actually live together as man and wife. Only three days later, Dick caught Evelyn in a compromising position with a man named William Bohozuk. There was a row, but somehow things were patched up — at least long enough for Evelyn and John Dick to move into a house at 32 Garrick Avenue on October 31, a house Evelyn had purchased.

But that rocky start was a sign of things to come. Dick showed up at Bohozuk's place of work and begged him to stay away from Evelyn. Though Bohozuk was not happy about Dick's visit, he decided to stop seeing Evelyn immediately after he found out she was married.

Certainly neither of Evelyn's parents liked Dick, saying he was always asking them for money. For his part, Dick had discovered that Donald MacLean was stealing from the Hamilton Street Railway and threatened to expose him. (It was eventually estimated that MacLean stole between $200,000 and $250,000 from the company, a large sum of money in those days.)

Evelyn and John Dick finally separated for good on December 24, 1945, and he moved in with his cousin's family.

* * *

On March 6, 1946, Dick told Ann Kammerer that he was going out to meet his ex-wife before heading to his job later in the day. "He had on a blue striped shirt and a navy blue suit and a blue sleeveless pullover," Kammerer said later, recalling that day. "He was wearing a short coat and a streetcar conductor's cap and black Oxfords."

Dick told Ann that Evelyn's attitude towards him had changed, and that she was now being very friendly. He explained that they had met the previous week and she had driven him over the mountain and had then produced some liquor for them to share. While he'd become suspicious and did not have anything to drink, Evelyn did. Dick had had to drive her home and carry her inside. Then, because he knew she didn't own a car, he'd written down the vehicle's licence number.

Nevertheless, it seems that Dick was willing to meet with her again.

* * *

Four police officers, including Detective Charles Wood and Clarence Preston, paid a visit to Evelyn at the Garrick Avenue house on March 19, search warrant in hand.

Wood said to Evelyn, "You have probably read in the paper the finding of a torso on the mountainside." She did not answer. When he then said, "The torso has been identified as the body of your husband," her attitude immediately changed and she replied, "Don't look at me. I don't know anything about it."

In their search of Dick's effects they found the slip of paper on which he'd written the licence number of the car Evelyn had been using. As the judge in the subsequent trial noted in a summation of the case, the car turned out to be a Packard sedan, owned by a William Grafton "who stated that he loaned the car to Mrs. Evelyn Dick from time to time and that she had it on the afternoon of March 6th, from 1:30 p.m. to 7:30 p.m. and when it was returned, the slip cover and rug were missing from the front seat and the car was bloodstained inside, and very muddy outside. A tie and blue woollen sweater were also found in the car, which were later identified as belonging to John Dick. Both articles were bloodstained and the sweater had a bullet hole in the right chest."

The officers took Evelyn down to the police station, where she admitted she had used the car in question on March 6, and had left a note for Grafton about the blood, saying that "the little girl had a bleeding."

Even after being warned by Wood that anything else she said might be used against her, Evelyn agreed to talk. Her lying alter ego was in full force as she described Dick as a philanderer who had been threatened a number of times by angry husbands. The next story she told was that a "gang from Windsor" had been out to avenge Dick's abuse of one of their wives. According to Evelyn, she'd been ordered to drive them up the mountain, where they had thrown Dick's remains out of the car.

While Evelyn was being interrogated, other officers were still searching her home. Besides a photograph of William Bohozuk, they found a man's watch and chain, a money changer, and a ticket punch — all bloodstained and having belonged to John Dick. Most damning of the discoveries, however, was what lay in the coal furnace in the basement. Sifting through the ashes, the officers uncovered bone fragments and the stump of a human tooth.

Evelyn was charged with vagrancy, used in those days to hold a suspect in jail until a more serious charge could be laid. She was held overnight in a police cell and arraigned the next morning.

While holding Evelyn, the police also brought Bohozuk in for questioning. As soon as Evelyn saw him she said she wanted to amend her statement from the previous day. She claimed that Bohozuk had borrowed $200 from her as a down payment on having John Dick murdered by "the gang." A week later, she added, Bohozuk had given her back the $200, telling her the gang was too busy to do the job. Bohozuk told the police he had indeed borrowed $200, but for another purpose. He also said he'd paid Evelyn back out of a bank loan he'd secured.

Confronted with the evidence found in the ashes, Evelyn agreed this time to give police "the whole story." Bohozuk and the gang, she claimed, had killed Dick and had then phoned her to tell her and borrow the car. She also said they had given her a paper bag with Dick's watch and other belongings because they'd thought she might like to have them.

* * *

There was still one more grisly discovery to be made.

On March 22, officers returned to the Garrick Avenue house to hunt for more evidence of murder. They found it — but not for the murder they had in mind. This time their search turned up the mummified corpse of a small baby.

In the attic, a locked beige suitcase caught the officers' attention. Breaking the lock open with a screwdriver, they immediately noticed a bad smell. A burlap bag was packed inside, and in that was a small wicker basket holding a cardboard box. The box held a chunk of rough cement with bits of clothing sticking out. The suitcase was taken to the police station and Dr. Deadman was called in.

The officers chipped away at the cement, exposing a skirt wrapped around a zippered leather shopping bag. In the bag was the decomposed body of a child "doubled up and forced into [it]," Deadman later testified. A tailor's label on the khaki skirt showed the name of E. MacLean. (The skirt was later shown to be the same one Evelyn had worn in her Red Cross photo.) Mixed through the cement were fragments of cloth, paper, and cardboard. According to Detective John Freeborn of the Hamilton Police, he had found an open bag of cement and a trowel during a search of Donald MacLean's home. Neither of these items ever turned up in the Garrick Avenue house.

Deadman attempted to do an autopsy on the partially mummified body, which began to crumble when he touched it. He was, however, able to identify it as being that of a boy younger than three weeks old. On the corpse was a diaper held by two rusty safety pins, a cotton shirt, and an infant's dress and wool sweater. Around the neck Deadman found a piece of heavy string.

Confronted with the discovery of the baby's corpse, Evelyn — contradicting previous statements she had made concerning her relationship with Bohozuk — confessed it was a child she'd had with Bohozuk in 1944, and that he had strangled it to death. At that point, both Evelyn and Bohozuk were formally charged with the murder of the baby, and Bohozuk was charged with the murder of John Dick.

Following the discovery of the baby, the police also searched Donald MacLean's home. There they unearthed two shotguns, a deer rifle, and a .22 rifle, none of which had recently been fired — but a .32 calibre revolver found in MacLean's bedroom had. The police also discovered a muddy pair of black Oxford shoes, later identified as belonging to Dick, with drops of blood on them. And on top of all that, officers found $4400 in bills, thousands and thousands of unused streetcar tickets, and a set of keys that could open the fare box of any streetcar or bus in the Hamilton system. MacLean was arrested and charged with the theft of streetcar tickets and cash.

But Evelyn had not run out of stories yet. She now implicated her father in Dick's death, saying he had loaned a gun to Bohozuk and had paid him $3000 to $4000 to kill Dick. Both Donald and Alexandra MacLean were then charged, in addition to Bohozuk, with Dick's murder.

The preliminary hearing took place from April 24 to 26, 1946. (It was at this hearing that the existence of Evelyn's "little black book" — which listed all the well-known men of Hamilton she had slept with — emerged. Under pressure during questioning, she mentioned "a magistrate's son," and the court abruptly ordered that the names of the men not be published in the papers.) As a result of the hearing, Evelyn, her father, and Bohozuk were all committed for trial. Evelyn's mother was freed of the charge.

Evelyn's trial for the murder of John Dick began October

7, 1946, amid tremendous excitement and media attention. A great deal was made of the "femme fatale" and her incredible beauty and shapely legs. Adults and children alike struggled to get a look at her as she arrived in court each day, and descriptions of what she was wearing were often published in the papers. Evelyn loved it all.

As far as the actual trial was concerned, the most damaging evidence came from the Crown's reluctant witness, Alexandra MacLean, who was under bond and forced to testify against her daughter. It seemed everything she said pushed Evelyn closer to the hangman's noose.

Alexandra recalled for the court that it was a beautiful afternoon on March 8 when she'd decided to take her granddaughter, Heather, for a walk. "I knew it was about time for John Dick's [streetcar] to come along. He always sounded the bell or the gong for Heather and she would wave her hand."

Alexandra said she was surprised when the car came and Dick was not on it. When she returned home she mentioned it to Evelyn, who apparently responded, "Well, it is not likely he will trouble me again, and you will never see him on a car."

Alexandra asked her daughter if something had happened to John.

"Yes, John Dick is dead, and you keep your mouth shut," her daughter replied.

Two days later, Evelyn suggested her mother take Heather for another walk. They left Evelyn alone in the house for two hours.

Later questioned about how the household disposed of the ashes from the coal furnace, Alexandra explained, "We used to put them out every Friday night and they were collected Saturday morning." However, she testified, she saw Evelyn removing the ashes from the basement on Wednesday, March 13, and spreading them around on the driveway in front of the garage. When Alexandra offered to help, Evelyn adamantly refused.

Evelyn's own statements to police were just as damaging, and her lawyer, John Sullivan, tried to keep them out of the trial on the basis that she had made them while she was facing a charge of vagrancy, not murder. He also maintained that some of her statements had been induced, not given of her own free will. The prosecutor, Timothy Rigney, argued that all Evelyn's statements had been voluntary, and Justice E.H. Barlow agreed with him. Although she never testified directly at her trial, all of Evelyn's various confessions and statements to the police were read into evidence.

It took the jury only 1 hour and 52 minutes to return its verdict: guilty, with a recommendation for mercy. Evelyn was sentenced to hang on January 7, 1947, but an appeal was promptly launched.

It was at this point that lawyer J.J. Robinette was brought on to defend Evelyn in the now very high-profile case. Ontario Deputy-General Cecil Snyder appeared in court with prosecutor Timothy Rigney to oppose the motion for a new trial.

Robinette, however, argued that Justice Barlow had been wrong in admitting into evidence Evelyn Dick's statements to police. He also argued that Barlow had made some vital errors in his charge to the jury. So well did he argue that the five-judge panel finally granted Evelyn a new trial — and with Robinette now defending her, the verdict in that trial came back "not guilty."

Evelyn had survived two trials for the murder of her husband, largely because it seemed unclear about whether she had taken an active or a passive role in the deed. There was no such uncertainty, however, about her guilt in the death of the 10-day-old baby.

The little boy had been born to Evelyn on September 5, 1944. It was her third child: in addition to Heather, born more than three years before Evelyn had met John Dick, Evelyn had given birth to a still-born daughter a year later. In those days, a great deal of stigma was attached to illegitimate children. Therefore, when Heather was born in 1942, Evelyn had made up a father for the birth certificate. She'd said she was married to a Norman White, who was on active duty in the Royal Canadian Navy. Pregnant again in 1944, she had fine-tuned the story. Not only was she married to someone in the navy, but he was lost at sea.

Evelyn's father had been very unhappy about the impending birth of this third child. Alexandra MacLean admitted that not long before Evelyn had left for the hospital, Donald had told his daughter not to bring the baby into the house.

"One baby in the house is enough," he was quoted as saying.

In the early hours of September 5, 1944, Evelyn had given birth to a healthy nine-pound baby boy. She'd named him Peter David White. Alexandra had visited mother and baby in the hospital, bringing a beige suitcase with some clothes for Evelyn and the baby.

Evelyn had returned home on September 15, alone. When Alexandra had asked her about the baby, Evelyn said it had been taken to the Children's Aid Society to be put up for adoption.

Childcare specialist Dr. Frank Boone later testified that he'd seen the newborn in the hospital and that the baby had been in excellent health. Although he'd wanted to see the infant again the day Evelyn had been due to check out of the hospital, she'd left before he could. Boone also said that a letter he'd sent her about a feeding formula — to an address she had given him — had been returned unopened. Evelyn's own doctor, Douglas Adamson, testified that he'd seen her alone on October 5 and 26, and that on both visits she'd told him the baby was fine.

And perhaps no one would ever have been the wiser about the fate of little Peter David White if his body had not been found in a suitcase.

On the same day an indictment for murder was brought against Evelyn in the case of John Dick, one was also brought against her for the death of her son. That trial began March

24, 1947. Once again she was defended by J.J. Robinette. In his closing arguments, he said that "according to biblical standards she is not a good woman, but that doesn't mean she's a murderess."

Judge A.M. Lebel agreed, saying to the jury, "This is a question, gentlemen, of murder, not of morals." However, he also clearly believed Evelyn had killed her child, adding, "What strikes me to be most important of all — in what suitcase were the remains of a child found?"

The jury was out for more than five hours before it returned its verdict: not guilty of murder, guilty of manslaughter. The following day the judge sentenced Evelyn to life for the murder of her son. She ultimately served only 12 years before being released on a "ticket-of-leave" (the predecessor to parole).

William Bohozuk was found not guilty in both murders, but was hounded for many years by the public. He married and had a family, finally changing his name to protect them.

Donald MacLean pleaded guilty to being an accessory after the fact in the murder of John Dick and was sentenced to five years in a penitentiary. He later received another five years, to run concurrently, for the thefts from the Hamilton Street Railway. In all, he served four years before being paroled in 1951 at the age of 74.

It was an unprecedented move, but when Evelyn finally left prison in 1959 she was treated as though she was in the witness protection program. The authorities told her that the only hope she would have of living a normal life would be to take on a new identity. They gave her one.

With her new name and a job, Evelyn walked into hiding and never returned. It was reported that she married well and that her new husband and those in her social circle didn't know who she really was. Hundreds of rumours circulated over the years about what happened to her and where she was living, but nothing was ever publicly confirmed. Once, many years after her release from prison, a meeting was arranged between Evelyn and the grown-up Heather, who by then had a child of her own. Although reportedly glad to have seen her daughter after so many years, Evelyn refused to give Heather a way to contact her again.

* * *

Plays, books, and numerous articles have been written about Evelyn Dick. Speculation about her can be narrowed down to two unalterable facts. Even if she did not pull the trigger herself, she was guilty of the murder of John Dick, acquittal or not. And the life of a little boy was ended before it had hardly begun.

Chapter 5
Truth and Consequences

It was, as Phoebe Campbell first recalled, shortly before midnight on Friday, July 14, 1871, when she awoke and became aware of two strangers in the room. She couldn't make out much in the darkness, but she clearly heard one of the intruders shout at her husband George, "Your money or your life!"

When George replied that they had no money, the intruder aimed a pistol at his head and pulled the trigger. All Phoebe heard was a click. The gun would not fire and it was thrown to the ground.

Then, said Phoebe, George sprang up in bed and one of the men grabbed him. George cried for her to bring him the axe. She did so, but one of the men snatched it from her just as George managed to get to his feet. "My husband was struck with the axe almost as soon as it was taken away from me," she later explained.

The blow didn't knock him down, but he screamed when he was struck, and yelled at Phoebe to get the butcher's knife. This, too, she said she managed to do, but one of the men again took the weapon away from her before she could give it to George. "He called for me to help him but I could not ... I could hear several blows of the axe; he was struck once after he fell and then it was perfectly quiet."

Phoebe initially claimed that "the two men were black and talked 'darky'," but then added that by the dim lights they were carrying she could see they were white men with faces they had blackened themselves. Nevertheless, she continued to refer to the killers as two black men. She said they were shorter than her husband, wore dark clothes, and made no sound when they walked, which made her think they were barefoot.

"I did not try to get out of the house because the children screamed and I could not leave them," she explained. Both three-year-old Mary Ann and a 10-month-old son witnessed the brutal slaying.

After ransacking the place looking for money, the intruders threatened Phoebe just before they left: "The two men swore that if I put my head out of doors before daylight, they would murder me."

Phoebe Campbell, widowed at 24, waited an hour and then sounded the alarm.

* * *

A small, stout woman of considerable strength, Phoebe had been married to George for four years. The couple had recently moved into the small log cabin, not quite six kilometres from the village of Thorndale, Ontario, in what was then the Township of West Nissouri.

It was 1:40 a.m. when Phoebe's nearest neighbour, Hugh Macdonald, heard her yelling. "The first words I could understand were her crying 'murder' and 'come quick,'" he later recalled. "She also cried, 'Is there any person going to hear me tonight?'"

In the heavy fog that had descended, Macdonald went to rouse two other neighbours, Richard Blackmore and William Craig, before venturing to the Campbells' cabin. When they arrived, they found Phoebe sitting outside holding Mary Ann. "Poor George was murdered," Macdonald recalled her saying. And she told them that two black men had been there and had "cut him all to pieces with the axe."

Phoebe described the horrible struggle and violent outcome of what had happened in the cabin. The long "tussle" between George and the two intruders had covered the entire one-room cabin, she said, and at one point they fell onto the trundle bed containing the children.

"She said the children began to cry and she went and took up the youngest and ... she then sat on the trundle bed and nursed it while the struggle continued," Macdonald later stated. Oddly, she also "spoke of regretting what had taken place."

The three neighbours went to the door of the cabin, lit a match, and looked inside. They could see George's body lying on the floor, but they did not enter. Phoebe went in, however, and brought out the baby, handing him to one of the men. She then took Mary Ann's hand and walked her along the path to the road. She repeatedly told the little girl that "two black men had killed her pa."

William Craig took the young family first to his place and then to the home of Phoebe's father, Joseph McWain. The other men roused the local residents and went to fetch the constable. The Campbells' closest neighbour, Thomas Davis, took 15 minutes to come to the door — a fact that would soon be used against him.

A coroner's jury viewed the body later on the Saturday, and by Sunday the brutally hacked and disfigured remains of "poor George" (as Phoebe now constantly called him) were laid out in a coffin at the Campbells' cabin. The funeral took place later that day as horror, revulsion, and anger quickly swept through the region. More than 1000 people swarmed into Thorndale, congregating around the scene of the crime, and at Rhan's Saloon, where endless theories were debated. A rumour began circulating that George had had a large sum of money temporarily in his possession, and that it was this money that had prompted his murder.

Detective Phair of the Ontario Provincial Police already had one suspect in custody — the tardy Thomas Davis. Phair escorted the suspect through a part of the mob that had gathered in town, and Davis begged the detective to get him away from there, for he feared being lynched. Davis explained to a *Globe and Mail* reporter that he suffered from very bad epileptic fits, and that he'd had one the night of the murder. He also explained that when his neighbours had knocked on his door that night he had still been in the "stupid condition" he experienced after a fit.

A search of Davis's residence on the Sunday, however, revealed a pile of recently washed clothes, still wet, with obvious bloodstains on them. Since Monday was typically laundry day in those parts, wet clothes on a Sunday immediately aroused suspicion. Davis's explanation that he had been killing chickens was not believed, and he was arrested and held for eight days, until the resumption of the coroner's inquest. Because Davis's father-in-law, John Priestly, had been with him that night, he too was arrested a few days later on suspicion of being an accomplice.

On July 19, yet another man, John Barry, was arrested and held for questioning regarding the murder. Barry was George Campbell's friend, and had apparently voiced concerns about the isolated location of the cabin. ("Some night you will be killed if you live there," he'd reportedly told George.)

In spite of these three arrests, the Township Council of West Nissouri posted a $500 reward for anyone who could help police find the killer or killers.

On the same day that John Barry was arrested, Detective Phair took Phoebe to nearby London by buggy so that she could make a deposition on the murder. Her father and her brother Hugh went there to pick her up and bring her home. All three, however, were ordered to return to London, where they were arrested on July 21 and held for further questioning. Perhaps in retaliation for her arrest, Phoebe charged Detective Phair with indecently assaulting her on the road to London on July 19. (The charges were later dropped.)

On July 22, Phoebe's first cousin, John McWain, was also arrested and held for questioning. Shortly after that, Thomas Coyle, a 19-year-old man who worked for Phoebe's father, was arrested after he was tentatively identified as the man who had purchased the malfunctioning pistol in St. Mary's a week before the murder.

That brought to eight the number of people in custody for having played some part in the murder of George Campbell.

* * *

The coroner's inquest, suspended the day after the murder, resumed on July 27. That morning, Davis, Priestly, and Barry were all released from jail and from suspicion. The 18-member coroner's jury heard all the evidence in private. Some details leaked out, however, and it was now generally believed that George had been murdered by someone within his extended family.

Phoebe's sister-in-law testified at the inquest that she had never heard a harsh word from George to his wife. The only dissension she'd seen centred on the fact that George's father had owed them money for the three years George had worked under him, and Phoebe had pushed George to get a note for the money, which he finally did. Perhaps because Thomas Coyle had lived with George and Phoebe when they'd resided in her father's house, rumours of impropriety between Phoebe and Coyle also surfaced. However, a number of witnesses made a point of saying there was nothing between the two.

The verdict from the inquest on August 4, 1871, was succinct: "We the jury, empanelled to investigate the death of one George Campbell, after viewing the body and hearing the evidence, have come to the conclusion that George Campbell was murdered by two persons whom we believe to be Thomas Coyle and Phoebe Campbell."

This was not an indictment, however, and the investigation into the murder continued. Her father and brother were both released from jail after the inquest, but Phoebe was kept in custody. Later that day she asked to see Mr. Hutchinson, the county Crown attorney. She said she wished to make a new statement about the night of the murder because her conscience was bothering her.

"My husband and I went to bed at 11 o'clock. We were asleep, the baby and I, in the back part of the bed," Phoebe said. "I was awakened by my husband calling out. I heard someone strike my husband in bed ... He called for the knife and I got it. The man called out, 'Don't fetch it here or I'll murder you too!' I knew the voice to be that of Thomas Coyle ...Coyle then struck him with the axe.

"He told me what to say afterwards and I did," she continued. "I was afraid to tell the truth because Coyle said if I told on him I would be hanged too."

After making her new statement, Phoebe requested to see her father at once. She also went to see Coyle in his cell, and told him what she had done. A witness to the meeting said that Coyle was more amused than upset.

It seemed the case was finally over, so it was a surprise to everyone the following day when Phoebe completely recanted her confession.

George, she said, had appeared to her in a vision the previous evening and had told her, "Phoebe, you're innocent and the blame of my death does not rest on the poor boy [Coyle] downstairs."

She would, she promised, *now* tell the truth. "The first I knew was an axe striking my husband and he screamed," Phoebe testified in court as the investigation into the murder continued. "After my husband screamed, [the man] struck him again with the axe. I did not see the axe. I could hear it. It was dark in the house and I could not tell who it was … The man says, 'I owe your husband a revenge. I would have shot him in his bed but the pistol would not go off.'"

Phoebe claimed that she'd asked, "Is that you John?" referring to her first cousin, John McWain. Telling the court that John had answered yes, she then continued with her story: "I said, 'What did you ever murder George for?' He says, 'When I was in Stratford gaol, your husband abused my wife.'"

Much of the story Phoebe then told was similar to her previous ones. By this time, however, she had told so many different stories it was hard to know what the truth was. Her sister, Mrs. McGufferin, went to the jail to see her.

"Oh Phoebe," she reportedly said. "Who would have ever thought of seeing you here?"

At that, Phoebe's composure broke and she sobbed deeply. There were so many "fearful stories going around about it" that Mrs. McGufferin said she wanted to hear the truth herself.

"I know I have told many lies about it," Phoebe answered, "but yesterday I did tell the truth and by that I intend to stick." When told that her many contradictory statements had created "a great feeling against herself," Phoebe replied, "I suppose I shall have to suffer for it … I suppose I'll be hanged for it."

John McWain denied everything Phoebe had said about him, including the part about the alleged intimacy between

George and his wife. He said George was always "well conducted and respected."

When the investigation into the murder continued on August 18, John McWain was front and centre. Phoebe was also recalled to the stand. The most interesting aspect of that day was an exchange in open court between her and her cousin.

McWain asked her why she was lying. Phoebe protested and then referred to the supposed motive. "My husband went to chop wood for your missus, and he told me he either went to bed with your wife, or as much as that he did."

"Now, Phoebe, you know you are swearing my life away falsely." McWain replied.

"You know you have done it, John, and there's no use you denying it. If you think to deceive your fellow creatures on earth, you cannot deceive the Lord," she said.

"I think you had better repent yourself," McWain warned his cousin. "You've more need to do so than I have."

At the end of the investigation, Phoebe and Thomas Coyle remained in jail, held on suspicion of murder. McWain was released on his own recognizance until the fall court session. During that session, charges of murder were filed against Phoebe and Coyle and their trials were postponed until spring 1872. No charges were filed against John McWain and he was officially off the hook.

* * *

Life in the region returned to normal until April 1, 1872, when Phoebe Campbell went on trial for her life in London, Ontario. Kenneth McKenzie was hired for the prosecution and Frank Cornish and Edmund Meredith for the defence. Phoebe herself was described as being dressed in mourning and having a "ruddy hue" on her cheeks. Her hair was in two long braids down her back and she appeared cool and very self-possessed. The crowd wanting to get in was anything but that.

While the jury was being sworn, the crowd outside — chiefly "boys and men of the rougher class" — forced their way through the doors of the building and rushed the court. They were falling over each other to grab every available seat and standing spot. The judge was horrified. Threatening to have some of them arrested, he said, "Rushing into a court of justice, as into a circus, upon such an occasion as the trial of a person for her life, [is] disgraceful."

The first couple of days of the trial saw a succession of witnesses who had come to Phoebe's aid on the night of the murder. They all testified they had heard her story of two black men killing George. As they did so, a picture slowly emerged of the carnage that had occurred in the log cabin that night. The witnesses described in detail what the murder scene had looked like when they'd walked in.

George had been seen lying on his back with his head towards the door of the one-room cabin. His feet were under the bed. What remained of his head was turned to the left and there was a great deal of blood under it. The blood-soaked axe was lying next to his body and a pistol was found under his shoulder. The right hand of his body was covered in blood and partially severed. There was some blood on the small trundle bed where the little girl slept, but little on the large bed except on one of the pillows. Dr. Charles Moore, having done the official examination for the coroner, stated that "the body did not fall out of the bed in the position (on the floor) that I saw it."

"The deceased did not receive any of the blows while in bed," Moore continued. "The head was mashed like jelly. The brains were actually knocked out. There were six or seven blows to the skull, which were made with the head of the axe. The blows could not have been given in the dark. I have no doubt there was a violent struggle."

Moore said the large cut on George's right wrist would have rendered the arm useless, and that there were also cuts on the left wrist. The large cut across George's throat was made around the time of death.

As the doctor described his brutal findings, Phoebe was visibly upset and kept her face covered with her handkerchief.

Almost everything in the cabin had been spattered with blood. It was on the logs of the cabin, the floor, and the door. The axe, which was discovered lying next to the body, was covered in blood; some of George's hair and scalp were still attached to it as well. Some of his whiskers were stuck in a large gash — made by the axe — in the front door, which also showed a handprint in blood. Dresses hanging up on the door had blood on them. According to neighbour Richard Blackmore, even a tin dish with salt in it showed heavy drops of blood.

"The house," said Blackmore, "looked as if there had been a struggle from one place to another."

A detective on the scene a couple of days after the murder had stepped on a piece of paper in the cabin. He'd noticed some blood on it and had picked it up. It was a sheet of paper from "a sermon on the cleaning of the sins of mankind with blood."

In a number of later statements, Phoebe had said she'd never touched George after the murder, but most of the witnesses from that night testified that her hands had had a great deal of blood on them — the reason she gave was that she had held George's head after the attack.

It was not only her conflicting comments and stories that were causing serious trouble for Phoebe's defence. A number of those testifying said when they looked at the scene of the murder, they were convinced that half of the bed had not been slept in — the half that Phoebe herself said she and the baby had occupied that night. The testimony of two witnesses in particular contradicted her descriptions of a fierce and long struggle between George and his assailants.

"I helped to wash all but the back of the deceased," neighbour William Craig testified. "His brother was with me. I noticed there was very little blood on his feet, and on the soles of his feet there [was] none."

This was confirmed by George's brother. With all the blood everywhere, if there had been a huge struggle, it would have been impossible for George not to have some blood on the soles of his feet.

By the third day of the trial, Phoebe realized things were not looking good at all. It was apparent she had not slept well and her cheeks were very pale. She kept her veil down, and her face was often buried in her handkerchief.

To many it had seemed that George and Phoebe had a solid and friendly relationship. "Campbell and my daughter lived on remarkable agreeable terms," her father said. "He was kind to her and she to him."

This was confirmed by numerous witnesses, as was the fact that Phoebe was a gentle, quiet, and hardworking woman.

Evidence against Phoebe included reported disagreements she'd had with George over some promissory notes. One was a note given to George by his father for work the former had done over the course of three years. It was supposed to be for $500, but John Campbell had deducted money for food and other items he had given George and Phoebe while they had lived in his house. Phoebe had been disappointed to discover the note was only payable to George, who'd promised his wife he would leave the note to her in his will. She had been putting pressure on George to collect the money owing. She had no way of knowing that George had given his father back the promissory note eight weeks before the murder.

A female prisoner who shared a cell with Phoebe testified that before the infamous vision of George, Phoebe had mentioned that John McWain, not Thomas Coyle, was the real killer of her husband. "She also said she felt very unhappy until she could write to Coyle to apologize for accusing him wrongfully of killing her husband," the prisoner continued. "She said if Coyle should be hung by her accusing him she hoped she would be hung beside him."

Another motive that surfaced during the trial was the possible relationship between Phoebe and Thomas Coyle. However, no one ever saw anything of an intimate nature take place between the two, and Coyle stated that "there never was any improper intimacy between me and the prisoner."

Phoebe had written him at least four letters, but they had been intercepted before they'd reached their destination and were later put into evidence. Coyle testified at the trial that he could neither read nor write.

Finally, near the close of the trial, it was also pointed out by two witnesses that it would have taken "a very strong man" to make some of the axe marks that scarred the floor and the door of the cabin. The question of whether Phoebe was strong enough to have committed this murder was raised but never answered.

The jurors, however, didn't take long to make up their minds. In less than an hour, Phoebe was found guilty of murdering of her husband. According to the *Globe and Mail* on

April 8, 1872, she kept her composure until the judge said the words "hanged by the neck."

"She gave utterance to a piteous moan and a look of agonizing grief stole over her countenance," the paper reported. The courtroom was silent except for Phoebe's painful cry, and she had to be supported by two constables as she was taken away. She was sentenced to be hanged on June 20, 1872.

On May 18, knowing there was no hope left, Phoebe made one more long, written confession — this time apparently really, *really* telling the truth about what had happened.

She wrote that the problems with her husband had started with his parents, with whom Phoebe and George were living at the time. They'd wanted George to go to California, and Phoebe was completely against it. There were also quarrels over the promissory notes. Phoebe claimed that George was very possessive of her and that he never took her side against his parents or anyone else.

The couple soon moved back in with her father, she said, a household in which Thomas Coyle also resided. According to Phoebe, as she complained about how George was treating her, Coyle slowly began to take her side — and her heart. "He began to draw my love to him," she recorded in her confession, "and when I was in a passion I would say things I would be sorry for after when it would be too late."

Coyle offered to make her single so they could be together. Gradually, their talk turned to the method of murder. When poison was ruled out, Coyle said he would go into St. Mary's to buy a pistol and, after Phoebe and George had moved into their own cabin, he would come one night and shoot the sleeping man. A week before the murder, he went to town on the pretence of getting a haircut. A store owner in St. Mary's later tentatively identified Coyle as the man who had purchased a gun similar to the one found in the cabin. Phoebe made the bullets for the gun.

Coyle, Phoebe's confession went on, told her he crawled out the window hole and down the logs of the McWain home while everyone slept, and then headed to the Campbells' cabin. He carried the gun, but was concerned it would not work, so he asked Phoebe to keep the axe nearby. His fear about the gun was justified, as it did not go off. The axe and the butcher knife were going to have to do the job. This story would be the only one in which the knife would play a key role — something that was corroborated by Dr. Moore's testimony of when in the sequence of events the knife was used on George.

This was Phoebe's final version of how the murder played out: As his lover watched, Thomas Coyle aimed the gun at the sleeping figure in the bed and pulled the trigger. There was a click, and George began to stir. Knowing his victim was a full six inches taller than him, Coyle was very nervous and quickly reached for the axe.

"Coyle struck him and struck at him again," Phoebe wrote. "By that time my poor husband was out of bed and they both had a hard struggle around the room and my husband got the axe away ... Coyle called me to come and take the axe away. I went to them both and took hold of the axe handle and it was all [covered in] blood and my husband had hold with both hands.

"I let go and Thomas told me to get the butcher knife for him ... and he took the knife from my hand and cut [George's] throat and then my husband fell on the floor."

Her confession continued: "I've done and said a great many things when I was in a passion ... but I don't blame anybody but myself for my trouble for I was a married woman and ought to have known better and I deserve punishing just as much as Thomas Coyle and perhaps more for I have told so many lies about it and accused the innocent."

Coyle was later acquitted of murder. However, the point raised at Phoebe's trial, that it would have been be difficult for a woman to swing the axe with the force needed, made Phoebe's last confession at least plausible. But because Phoebe had told so many lies, the jury in Coyle's trial felt they could not convict him. Phoebe's father had also testified that Coyle could not have left the cabin that night without his knowledge.

On June 20, 1871, Phoebe went calmly to the scaffold after issuing a last letter to everyone telling them not to sin as she had done and asking for forgiveness.

Chapter 6
Did the Right Man Hang?

Little we know when morning skies are clearest,
what tempests may engulf the closing day.
Thomas D'Arcy McGee

In response to concerns for his well-being in March 1868, one of Canada's Fathers of Confederation, Thomas D'Arcy McGee, said there was no danger of his being converted into a political martyr. "If ever I were murdered," he pronounced, "it would be by some wretch who would shoot me from behind."

Only days later, someone would do just that.

Threats on McGee's life had become almost commonplace as 1867 drew to a close. It had been a groundbreaking year, both for Canada and McGee. He had been one of the 36 delegates to take part in conferences in Charlottetown, Quebec, and London, England, from 1864 to 1867. The

Thomas D'Arcy McGee, photographed in 1862 aged 37

resolutions passed at these meetings formed the basis for a federal union. They were written into the British North America Act, proclaimed July 1, 1867, creating the Dominion of Canada. These 36 delegates became known as the Fathers of Confederation. Ten of them — including Ireland's D'Arcy McGee — may have been born outside the country, but they were all Canadians when they started the push towards Confederation. McGee had represented Montreal West for some years (most of those as a federal cabinet minister) and, by the autumn of 1867, his political career was winding down. He would fight one last political campaign that fall.

As well as running for the new Dominion Parliament, McGee had decided to become a candidate for the Ontario provincial government in the County of Prescott. No rule at that time prevented a person from being a member of two legislatures. Lack of campaign funds, on the other hand, did begin to pose a problem for McGee. (He was not independently wealthy and money was always very tight for him and his family.) A few weeks into the Ontario campaign, he withdrew his candidacy. He would not have that same problem federally in Montreal, where his friends took care of the election expenses.

Standing just over five feet, two inches, McGee was short in stature but not in intellect or talent. In addition to being kind and generous — the latter in spite of his not having any money of his own — he was well known as a poet and writer, and much of what income he did earn came from that vocation. He was also one of the most eloquent and engaging speakers in the history of Canadian politics. When he rose to speak, everyone listened.

McGee had been in poor health for some months, and in August 1867 he was confined to home. During that time, he wrote a series of scathing articles for the *Montreal Gazette* on the dangers and threat of Fenianism, a radical American-Irish movement.

One result of this series was that it gave him the voter support to win that first post-Confederation election in 1867, against a man named Bernard Devlin, a pro-Irish independence supporter. Gradually, as winter approached, McGee's strength began to return and he had every reason to believe that the year ahead, 1868, would be a good one. But the threats on his life had not abated.

One such threat in Montreal was reported to McGee by Alexander Turner, a Montreal constituent. "I told Mr. McGee on Notre Dame Street a week or fortnight after the election that there were persons accumulating at Scanlon's [Tavern] who, if they did not intend to take his life, they meant bodily harm to him," Turner later recalled. "He asked me if they were Irishmen who took an interest in Devlin. I said they were. He said he thought it was only the excitement about the election and it would die away but if I heard more about it to tell him."

McGee spent New Year's Day, 1868, at home with his family — his wife Mary, his two daughters, and his half-brother, John McGee. While one daughter played the piano, they all drank ginger beer, ate cake, and sang along. Afterwards, McGee stayed up reading until 1:00 a.m. and then went to bed. A half-hour later the family was all awakened by the front doorbell.

McGee's brother opened the door and saw two men. One of them said he wanted to see McGee about something. Though John commented on the lateness of the hour, the man was insistent. McGee agreed to see them, but told John to stand by him in case of need.

"I let one in," John McGee said later, "the other had then left. I brought him upstairs to the library where my brother was. I locked both doors and put the keys in my pocket when I went upstairs ... The man sat down and told my brother there was an attack to be made on the house that night at four o'clock. That he heard it from his friend, who was at a dance, but he could not give any names. He gave his own name as Smith of the Grand Trunk."

Meanwhile, McGee had told his brother to let in the other man, who was outside in the cold. John went to do so, but the man chose to stay in the shadows across the road and would not come in.

McGee quickly wrote a letter to the Superintendent of Water Police: "Information has been brought here of an intention to fire this house at 4:00 a.m. At this hour I cannot see the proper officer, but I request a guard of two men, or more if deemed necessary, to protect life and property."

At 1:45 a.m., McGee handed the letter to his visitor and asked him to deliver it to the police. The letter was delivered at 4:45 a.m. "Smith" told the officers that he had been directed to another police station first, hence his delay.

It wasn't until 5:30 a.m. that the police finally arrived at McGee's — but then, no one came to attack the house either.

The threats on McGee's life continued. Sir John A. Macdonald was very concerned and warned him to be careful.

In a letter to Macdonald, McGee thanked him for his warning and said he would not forget it. To his other friends and his family, McGee would simply say, "Threatened dogs live long."

By March 1868, McGee's health had improved enough to allow him to return to Ottawa for what he expected to be his last session in Parliament. With Confederation behind him and many political enemies in his path ahead, McGee knew his own time in government was coming to a close. Back in the capital, he moved into Toronto House, otherwise known as Mrs. Trotter's Boarding House. Located on Sparks Street, it was a short walk away from the Parliament Buildings on Wellington Street.

The skies were clear and the full moon bright on the evening of April 6, 1868. McGee returned to Mrs. Trotter's shortly after 7:00 p.m. and went to his room in search of papers he wanted to take with him to the House of Commons for the evening session. He had something important he wanted to say.

Robert McFarlane, another member of the House, was present when McGee spoke. "The subject of debate was the propriety of recalling Dr. [Charles] Tupper from England," he recalled. "Thomas D'Arcy McGee ... addressed the House that night on the question. I recollect a passage in the speech in reference to Dr. Parker who sat next to me in the House and moved the resolution.

"[McGee] spoke of the conduct of Dr. Parker attacking

Mr. Tupper when he was absent and could make no defence, that it was unmanly and un-English and was like hitting a man under the belt. He appeared in good health and spirits. He addressed the house with a good deal of animation and fire."

That night, McGee may well have been talking about himself, as much as Tupper, when he said: "It has been charged against him that he has lost the confidence of his own people. Sir, I hope that in this House mere temporary or local popularity will never be made the test by which to measure the worth or efficiency of a public servant. He, Sir, who builds upon popularity, builds upon shifting sand."

The evening was supposed to have ended at midnight, but business was not wrapped up until just after 2:00 a.m. Parliament was about to recess for the Easter break and most members — happy at the prospect of going home — were in a friendly mood. McGee asked McFarlane for help on with his coat.

"Mr. McGee asked me to go down to the saloon," McFarlane said later. "I did so and he took two cigars and I drank a glass of whiskey and water."

As the two of them walked out into the crisp night air, McGee, still suffering the bad leg that was a result of his illness, leaned on McFarlane's arm. He was wearing an overcoat, gloves, and a new white top hat. In his free hand was his wheat-coloured bamboo cane with a silver handle and engraved band.

Walking slowly, the two headed out the front gateway of

the Parliament Buildings to Wellington Street. Veering slightly to their left, they soon reached Metcalfe Street and walked one block south to Sparks Street. Here they parted. McGee was a mere 250 steps from home.

"Good night," McFarlane said.

McGee replied, "God bless you."

As McFarlane turned to head off, he noticed the parliamentary doorkeeper's brother, John Buckley, and three other men walking along. McGee had crossed to the south side of Sparks Street and was turning west.

"Good night, Mr. McGee!" Buckley called out.

"Good morning!" McGee answered. "It is morning now."

Those would be the last words he was heard to utter.

The sidewalks were a little icy, so McGee continued to walk slowly, the noise of his cane on the ice filling the darkness, and the smoke from his cigar filling the air. The opposite side of the street was bathed in moonlight but McGee walked in shadows. The gas street lamps were not lit — the city's contract with the gas company called for service only "during the dull period of the moon."

The stores on Sparks were closed, but lights were on in the *Ottawa Times* building across the street, where the printers were at work on the morning's issue.

Mrs. Trotter's house had three entrances. The first one led to a public bar (a common feature of boarding houses in those days). McGee passed by it and stopped in front of the second door, which led into the building's main hallway. He

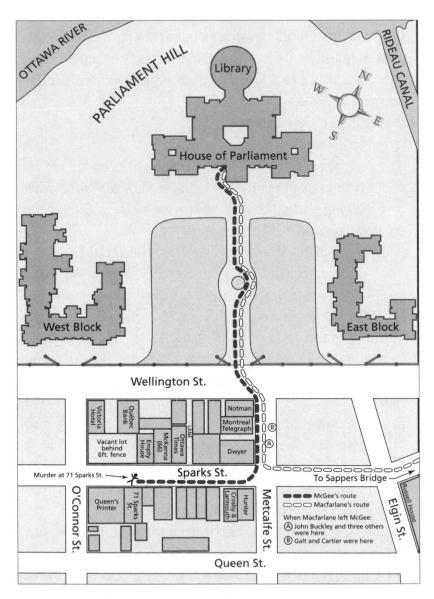

A map showing the route McGee took on his last night

removed a glove, took out his key, and put it in the lock.

"I always waited up ... until the members came from the House," Mrs. Trotter was to recall. "I heard a quick step passing the dining room window. I said to myself, 'That's my boy [her 13-year-old son was a page]; I will go and let him in.' I heard a noise as he was passing the window. I said, 'Be quiet. I will open the door for you.'... I opened the door leading from the dining room to the hall and then opened the hall door [to the street] a short distance, enough to let the boy in and the noise had then ceased.

"Finding he did not come in, I hesitated and wondered why. I pushed the door forward a little ... when the flash came across my face and I smelt the powder. I said that must be a fire cracker. I still held the door in my hand. I was not at all frightened. I went forward and saw a man stooping against the stone work of the house, on the right-hand side of the door leading into the house."

Mrs. Trotter was not carrying a lamp, so she went back into the dining room to get one, closing the door behind her. "I thought at the time the man had received a stroke which stupefied and knocked him against the house," Trotter continued. "I told my daughter there was someone hurt. I then took a lamp, opened the [dining room] door and found the blood scattered over the hall inside the door.

"When I opened the [front] door, the body seemed still against the wall and a little more stooped. The figure fell back on the side walk, the feet just at the door, quivered a little and then lay still. I then saw it was a dead man and I then gave the alarm."

She heard no footsteps of anyone running away, nor any voices. Her son, William Trotter, was walking home with two other House of Commons pages when he heard a shot. "I stood at the corner of Sparks and O'Connor looking towards the door of my mother's house. I saw something lying on the sidewalk. I thought it was a Newfoundland dog." He quickly realized it wasn't, and ran into the *Times* building to get help.

The assassin had held the gun close enough to singe McGee's hair, but not close enough to burn the skin, although the bullet did pass through the upper collars of the overcoat, undercoat, and shirt. The bullet entered just right of the spinal column, travelled through the upper part of the throat, and along the roof of the mouth. When it finally exited through the upper lip at the front, it took four of McGee's front teeth with it.

Dr. Donald Gillivray, the first doctor on the scene, arrived within minutes of being summoned. He found portions of McGee's teeth and cigar about 30 centimetres inside Mrs. Trotter's front hall, confirming the shot had been fired while she'd held the door open. McGee's body was lying face up across the wooden sidewalk, his head pointed towards the street and his feet resting about one metre from the door. His gloveless right hand was stretched out, while his other arm was bent at an awkward right angle, hooked by his cane, which was pinned under his back. Large quantities of blood oozed from his mouth and the wound at the back of his neck, spreading more than a metre across the planks of the sidewalk and into the gutter.

Gillivray noticed the key was still in the door, and lodged in the wood just above the latch was a lead pistol ball. The bullet later fell out, and Gillivray handed it to the coroner. The lower part of the door was covered with blood, which, Gillivray thought, "appeared to be thrown from above downward."

The doctor was only one of the many people who converged at the murder scene within minutes of it taking place. Someone had raced to Sir John A. Macdonald's house to notify him, and he had rushed over to the site. With the bottom half of McGee's face torn open and blood clotting his beard, it was obvious to all present that this had been a brutal end. Macdonald cradled his old friend's head as other men lifted McGee's body and carried it into the boarding house.

Thomas D'Arcy McGee was just days short of his 43rd birthday. His death became the first political assassination in the new Dominion of Canada.

* * *

Dawn was breaking as Macdonald left Mrs. Trotter's a few hours later. A light snow was falling onto the pools of blood still present on the sidewalk, and the city was very quiet. That soon changed as news of the murder spread.

In her diary on that day, Macdonald's wife, Agnes, recorded what everyone immediately assumed: "We felt at once that the shot was fired by a Fenian," she wrote.

The Great Famine in Ireland (1845–1848) reduced the Irish population by two million and the British received most of the blame. One movement, Young Ireland (of which McGee was then a member), wanted to sever all ties with Great Britain. The Repeal movement, by contrast, called for the repeal of the Act of Union that joined Ireland to Great Britain, but without severing all ties.

Thousands of Irish left the famine behind and moved to the United States, taking their beliefs in the movements with them. In their new country, anti-English feelings swelled among these Irish-Americans and gave rise to the Fenian organization (also known as the Irish Republican Brotherhood), a secret society that believed in armed revolution. D'Arcy McGee was not part of this.

In 1865, the Fenians decided to invade Canada. Their movement was rumoured to have as many as 60 chapters in the country at the time. As a precaution against a suspected attack, the federal government put out the call for militia volunteers in March 1866. Fourteen thousand men responded.

That April, a group of Fenians massed at Eastport, Maine, intending to invade Canada at Campobello Island, New Brunswick. They withdrew when they learned there was more opposition than they first expected. On May 31, 1866, however, 600 Fenians in New York State, under John O'Neill, marched almost 5 kilometres from Black Rock to Buffalo and crossed the Niagara River into Canada. They occupied Fort Erie, Ontario, cut telegraph lines, and proceeded inland. The volunteer militia was ordered out, but subsequently got driven back on June 2 by the Fenians at Ridgeway, Ontario. The invaders then retreated to Fort Erie and forced back another group of Canadians. By June 3 20,000 men had taken up arms to fight, but the Fenians had retreated to the United States, where they received a hero's welcome. Then, a few days later, the Fenians — their ranks now numbering 1000 — entered Canada again and occupied Pigeon Hill in Missiquoi County, Quebec. They were defeated only because American authorities seized their supplies.

At that point, the invasions stopped, but not the threat. McGee was more aware of this than anyone. He was a very outspoken critic of the Fenians and their militant ways. Whether they were responsible for his murder is a topic that has been debated ever since the morning of April 7, 1868.

* * *

The tributes for D'Arcy McGee poured in later that day in Parliament. As he rose to address the House, Sir John A. Macdonald was almost unable to speak. "It is with pain, amounting to anguish, that I rise to address you," he began. "He who last night, nay, this morning was with us, and of us, whose voice is still ringing in our ears, who charmed us with

his marvellous eloquence, enlivened us by his large states-
manship and instructed us by his wisdom and his patriotism,
is now no more — is foully murdered.

"If ever a soldier who fell on the field of battle, in front
of the fight, deserved well of his country, Thomas D'Arcy
McGee deserved well of Canada and its people ... To all the
loss is great. To me, may I say, inexpressibly so; as a loss not
only of a warm political friend ... but of one with whom I
enjoyed the intercommunications of his rich and varied
mind, the blow has been overwhelming.

"He might have lived a long and a respected life had he
chosen the easy path of popularity rather than the stern one
of duty," Macdonald continued. "Well, may I now say on
behalf of the Government and the country, that if he has fall-
en, he has fallen in our cause, leaving behind him a grateful
recollection, which will ever live in the hearts and minds of
this county.

"Then we must remember, too, that the blow which has
fallen so severely on this house and the country, will fall still
more severely on his widowed partner and his bereaved children. He was too good, too generous to be rich."

Macdonald then pledged that Canada would financial-
ly look after McGee's wife and children. Others
paying tribute to the slain man made not-so-subtle references to the Fenian movement. Pierre Chauveau, the first
premier of Quebec and federal member for Quebec County,
was one of these. "Great things are never done except at the

peril of the life of those who accomplish them," Chauveau said, addressing the House in French. "Nevertheless, [McGee's] patriotism made him disdain that danger, and the fear of that danger never caused him to recoil in the struggle which he had undertaken against those whose hand had struck him last night."

A round of thunderous "Hear, hear!" greeted his words. "That death is the baptism in blood of confederation, and the sacrifice of him who did so much to bring about that confederation."

While the assembly in the House of Commons was praising McGee and mourning his loss, the inquest into his death had started the same evening. By that time, six people had already been arrested in connection with the assassination. All were arrested without warning — no reasons given and no charges laid. As prisoners, and without counsel, they were obliged to answer questions under oath before a jury. Then, just after 11:00 p.m., they were all suddenly released, and someone else was taken into custody. The arrests continued, and soon the prison was filled with possible assassins.

By the time the investigation was over, five months later, more than a 100 people had been arrested in connection with the murder. One man, however, Patrick James Whelan, quickly became the prime suspect.

Not much is known about Whelan, except that he was born in Ireland and came to Canada via Quebec City. He spent two years there, serving with volunteers who, ironically, were guarding against Fenian raids. After that, he worked as a tailor in Montreal before marrying in 1867 and moving to Ottawa. Reportedly in his late twenties then, he liked going to the House of Commons to listen to the debates, which he did the night of the murder.

When arrested on the evening of April 7, Whelan had a Smith and Wesson revolver with him. It was not unusual at the time for men to carry weapons. A reporter for the *Globe and Mail* who interviewed Whelan in his prison cell shortly after his arrest wrote, "He is a bold, dashing, well-dressed fellow, with gold watch and chain, and very daring and self-possessed."

Whelan said the six-shooter revolver had been loaded some time before, although a girl in the house where he was staying picked it up once and accidentally fired it, wounding herself in the arm. The bullet in that chamber had been replaced.

* * *

The funeral in Montreal for McGee was held April 13, which would have been his 43rd birthday. More than 100,000 people either marched or gathered along the route to say goodbye. He was entombed at Côte des Neiges Cemetery, where his wife and two children said their private goodbyes. Mary McGee would never recover from the blow of losing her husband, and she died three years later.

The funeral procession at the corner of Bleury and Craig Streets

* * *

The investigation into McGee's murder continued. Rewards eventually totalling $14,000 were posted, even as the focus continued on Whelan, who had made no secret of his opposition to McGee's political ideologies.

As all other suspects were slowly eliminated, Whelan was charged with the murder. Three other men — Patrick Buckley, John Doyle, and James Kinsella — were charged as co-conspirators. Whelan and the three men all knew each other well.

Whelan's week-long trial took place in September 1868, with Judge William Richards residing. J. O'Reilly was the lawyer for the prosecution and J. Cameron, M. Cameron, and K. McKenzie were the lawyers for the defence. The latter three all received death threats for defending Whelan.

The trial began with a controversy during the jury selection. The defence challenged a witness who had publicly declared before the trial that he thought Whelan guilty. The judge disallowed the challenge, and the tone of the trial was set.

Most of the testimony centred on a few key issues. One was the Smith and Wesson revolver found on Whelan. The .32 calibre bullet found at the scene of the murder was a common type of bullet that could fit Whelan's gun. Forensic evidence was not yet available, so the focus was on the fact that the gun had been recently fired.

Confirming Whelan's story to the newspaper reporter, young Euphémie Lafrance testified at the trial to finding the gun in Whelan's room and accidentally discharging it. She even showed the court the wound on her arm.

However, that did not seem proof enough in light of the testimony from a Sergeant Davis. "I noticed the chambers of the revolver contained a cartridge different from the rest," said Davis at the trial, "which seemed to have been newly put in. You could easily shove it out. The others could not easily be removed ... I tried them all and found this was the only one that shoved out easily."

A supposed jailhouse confession from Whelan to another prisoner was another major blow to the defence. Because this confession was reportedly overheard by detective Andrew Cullen in an adjacent cell, it was treated as very credible evidence. The defence produced witnesses from other nearby cells, however, who said they heard no such confession, but in the courtroom their words were given no credence.

Also mentioned at the trial was the fact that Whelan was the man in question who had gone to McGee's house on New Year's night to warn him of an attack. When he was arrested and saw McGee's brother, John, at the jail, he introduced himself and reminded John that they had met at McGee's house that night. Again, the focus in the trial was not on his good intentions, but rather that he did not drop off the warning at the police station until 4:45 a.m.

The Crown's star witness was Jean-Baptiste Lacroix, a labourer who testified he witnessed Whelan kill McGee. When first questioned a few days after the murder, he said he'd only heard a shot, but his story changed several times in following statements, and he made several major errors in his testimony at the trial. For one, he stated that the killer was shorter than the victim. Whelan, however, was at least four and a half inches taller than McGee. In addition, McGee had not been wearing the black beaver hat that Lacroix claimed to have seen him in. Lacroix also had trouble identifying Whelan at

the jail, even though he said he'd seen the killer clearly —
despite the fact there had been no street lamps lit that night
and the murder had occurred on the side of the street in shadow. His explanation for why he had not gone to help the fall-
en victim was that he'd been afraid and had run away.

Lacroix had not voluntarily come forward to the police,
but was apparently tracked down by them. The holes in his
story raised plenty of questions about his credibility, and the
defence also called many witnesses to prove Lacroix was a
known liar and thief. In the end, however, it seemed that all
the jury heard was that he had seen the murder and identified Whelan as the assassin.

Whelan's wife attended the trial daily. On the fourth day,
Sir John A. Macdonald and his wife, Agnes, also arrived at the
courtroom and sat on the bench not far from the judge.
Though having promised to do so, the prosecution was never
able to prove that Whelan was a Fenian. (Many scholars in
the years since have combed through Fenian records and
nowhere does the name of Whelan appear.)

Despite the prosecution's extremely weak case, there
seemed little doubt as to the verdict. The newspapers had
been declaring Whelan guilty for weeks — and the jury followed suit on September 15, 1868.

Whelan had not been allowed to take the stand in his
own defence, but he had his opportunity to speak before the
judge passed sentence on him. He rose. "My Lord and
Gentlemen, I have been tried and found guilty, of course, of

the crime of murdering Hon. Thomas D'Arcy McGee," Whelan said, "and I protest, as I am about standing on the brink of the grave and must shortly appear at the bar of God. I swear to you before God almighty that I never committed that deed. I know this in my heart and soul well ... I have been accused by the counsel for the Crown of Fenianism. I can assure you and every loyal British subject in Canada that I never was a Fenian at home or abroad, that I never belonged to any organized body ..."

He also set the record straight about New Year's night, after it was revealed during the trial that he was the same man who had gone to the McGee house. "It was represented here to be a dance house," he said. "It was not such. I heard a conversation between two men there, who were shielded from me by a thin partition, and I heard one of them say that that night McGee's house would be burned. There was a man with me when I went to give the information at McGee's that night ... I swear solemnly I did not give my name as Smith, but my friend at the door gave that name.

"I am no Fenian. I would sacrifice the last drop of my blood for that noble woman [Queen Victoria] whose portrait I now see hanging before me in court. I served her nine years and six months in the army, four years of which time I served in India; when a man like me comes to speak of being called a black assassin, my blood runs cold at the thought. The man who was murdered was a man against whom I never had any spite. I know him to be talented and proud of his country, and I was proud of him ...

"I must say at the same time that if I was placed in the position of any one of the gentlemen of the jury, with such evidence brought against another man as they raked up against me, I would certainly bring in the same verdict as they have done, and I fully exonerate them from all blame whatever in the matter."

Patrick James Whelan was then sentenced to hang on December 10, 1868. His lawyers launched an appeal immediately, based on the faulty jury selection. All appeals were rejected. Whelan's execution was stayed twice, but finally he was to hang February 10, 1869.

On February 9, Whelan wrote a letter, which also bore the name of a lawyer and a witness. In it he said that, to his knowledge, Patrick Buckley and John Doyle knew nothing connected to McGee's murder (all three co-conspirators were ultimately acquitted).

The most interesting part of that letter was a postscript, also signed and witnessed: "To the foregoing statement I voluntarily add that I know the man who shot Mr. McGee."

In a conversation with his wife the day before his execution, Whelan confirmed this statement. He told her he was not guilty of the murder. He did not fire the shot — but he knew who did. When she asked why he wouldn't name the person to officials, Whelan replied that he would rather hang than be an informer.

At sunrise the next morning, the snow began to fall. By

10 a.m. a crowd of 5000 had gathered to watch what would be Canada's last public hanging. "A number of women settled comfortably under fur robes in their sleighs," the *Globe and Mail* reported.

The scaffold was erected at the top of the wall so that it could be seen by spectators, but also so the prisoner could be brought out through a window. Dangling from the scaffold's crossbeam and twisted loosely round a post was a hemp rope. Below the platform, the drop was hidden by the wall.

When the window opened and the hangman appeared, the crowd started shouting and small boys pelted him with snowballs. He loosened the rope and cleared off some snow before returning inside. In Whelan's cell, his arms were tied to his side and he was offered a drink. He refused.

Whelan was led out through the window and was heard reciting the Lord's Prayer. He then spoke to the crowd. "Friends and fellow countrymen," he said in a trembling voice, "for any offence I may ever have committed against any of you — I hope you will forgive me. I heartily forgive everybody who has ever injured me. From the bottom of my heart I ask forgiveness for same, the same for myself."

Whelan stopped and looked at the sky. "God save Ireland and God save my soul."

Father O'Connor touched a crucifix to his lips and the trap was sprung.

Whether by accident or on purpose, the noose was not tied correctly and Whelan's neck did not break. He strangled to death, and it took five minutes before his body stopped squirming. The wagon sent to pick up his body was turned away. Fearing his funeral would be used in Montreal as a huge pro-Fenian demonstration, the government decided Whelan would be buried secretly and at night in the grounds of the Ottawa jail yard. A priest would not officiate at the funeral because it was not consecrated ground. (Eventually the old jail became the Ottawa Youth Hostel. Many young travellers over the years have reported seeing Whelan's ghost.)

* * *

In 2002, 133 years after the hanging, descendents of Patrick James Whelan held a ceremony near the spot of the execution. A priest blessed the earth and placed some of it in a box, which was then taken to Montreal and buried next to Whelan's wife in Côte des Neiges Cemetery — the same cemetery where McGee is buried.

Whelan's descendents have also pushed for an inquiry into what they feel was a wrongful conviction and execution. They want his name (and theirs) cleared. It is clear that he never would have been convicted today on the evidence that sent him to the gallows in 1868.

Does Whelan deserve justice after all these years? Perhaps the last word should go to D'Arcy McGee:

*The dead have their rights as the living have; injustice
to them is one of the worst forms of all injustice.*

Bibliography

MacDonald, Cheryl. *Who Killed George? The Ordeal of Olive Sternaman.* Toronto, ON: Natural Heritage / Natural History, 1994.

Phelan, Josephine. *The Ardent Exile: The Life and Times of Thos. D'Arcy McGee.* Toronto, ON: Macmillan Canada, 1951.

Slattery, Timothy Patrick. *The Assassination of D'Arcy McGee.* Toronto, ON: Doubleday Canada, 1968.

Vallee, Brian. *The Torso Murder: The Untold Story of Evelyn Dick.* Toronto, ON: Key Porter, 2001.

Acknowledgments

I am always thankful to the writers who came before me, leaving a trail of history for me to follow in news clippings, magazine articles and books. I am grateful to all of you.

Thanks to my friend, Seema Shah, who always listens patiently to my tales of murder and intrigue. As with my first murder book, she made the process of writing this book so much easier.

To Janice Dowling — I really appreciate the work you did for the chapter on Olive Sternaman. The help was invaluable.

I want to sincerely thank the people at The National Archives of Canada in Ottawa. Their help, in person and later by phone, allowed me to quickly find the trial transcripts and other research material I needed.

A special note of thanks to all the court reporters of the past, whose diligence has allowed me to read exactly the words said during trials that took place more than a hundred years ago.

To my editor, Georgina Montgomery, for all her efforts and skills (and true understanding of how difficult it is for writers to part with any of their words!). I thank you for making me a better writer.

And many thanks to all the cats in my life who have supported both me and my writing — you know who you are.

Photo Credits

About the Author

Susan McNicoll lives in Vancouver, BC, where she divides her time between writing and running her own business doing bookkeeping and taxes. Although she is now a die hard British Columbian, her heart still belongs to the Toronto Blue Jays. Susan's lifelong love of words and history has been the main focus of her writing career, which began with five years as a reporter for the *Ottawa Journal* in the 1970s. She spent eleven years writing a book on post-war Canadian theatre history, which is scheduled to be published in 2004. She goes back to her home province for this second Amazing Stories murder book (her first, *British Columbia Murders*, was published in October 2003). Although her published work to date has been in the non-fiction realm, Susan is currently working on a series of fables based on the four seasons of healing.

OTHER AMAZING STORIES

These titles are available wherever you buy books. If you have trouble finding the book you want, call the Altitude order desk at **1-800-957-6888**, e-mail your request to: **orderdesk@altitudepublishing.com** or visit our Web site at **www.amazingstories.ca**

New **AMAZING STORIES** titles are published every month.